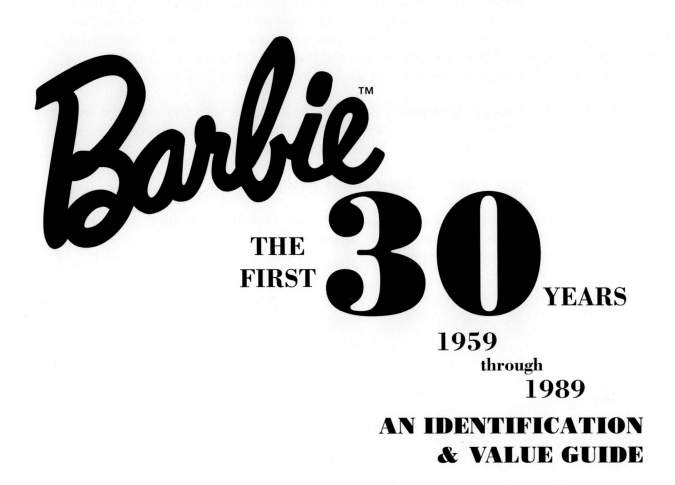

Barbie™

THE FIRST 30 YEARS

1959 through 1989

AN IDENTIFICATION & VALUE GUIDE

Stefanie Deutsch

COLLECTOR BOOKS

A Division of Schroeder Publishing Co., Inc.

Searching for a Publisher?

We are always looking for knowledgeable people considered to be experts within their fields. If you feel that there is a real need for a book on your collectible subject and have a large comprehensive collection, contact Collector Books.

On the Cover:

SuperStar Barbie, 1989 (see page 141);
No. 1 Barbie, 1959 (see page 22).

Cover design by Beth Summers

Book design by Terri Stalions

Additional copies of this book may be ordered from:
Collector Books
P.O. Box 3009
Paducah, Kentucky 42002-3009

or

Stefanie Deutsch
177 Telegraph Rd. #703
Bellingham, WA 98226

@$24.95. Add $2.00 for postage and handling.
Copyright: Stefanie Deutsch, 1996

Printed by IMAGE GRAPHICS, INC., Paducah, Kentucky

Contents

Acknowledgments

Barbie collectors are special. Here are a few names of Barbie doll friends who were of tremendous help and encouragement and made (and make) collecting so much fun: David Berry, Joe Blitman, Gail Dunn, Sarah Eames, Betina Evers, Sandra Goss, Edna Hoffman, Franklin Lim Liao, Eric Lucas, Jo McBride, Simone Neumann, Michele Quintana, Georgia Seibel, Carda Starcke, Francois Theimer, Sumiko Watanabe, and Janet Winterflood.

About the Author

Stefanie Deutsch started collecting Barbie dolls in 1980 when she was still attending school in Germany. Her collection grew quickly and she became well known through the German press, radio, and TV. In 1986 she formed an official Barbie doll collector club for Germany, Austria, and Switzerland. She still serves as president of this club. In 1989 for Barbie doll's 30th anniversary her dolls were shown in major, Mattel organized, exhibitions all over Germany and Switzerland. After graduating from law school with honors Stefanie and her family (including some thousand Barbie dolls) emigrated to America. Here, in 1992, she wrote her first book about Barbie dolls, a price guide published in Germany that is now in its second printing. Stefanie is currently president of "Barbie Doll and Friends of Vancouver."

If you should have any questions about Barbie, Stefanie would be happy to help you (please include a self addressed stamped envelope). Her address is:

Stefanie Deutsch
177 Telegraph Rd. #703
Bellingham, WA 98226

No other doll has taken the hearts, of children and collectors alike, by storm like Barbie, the number one toy in the world. This doll in her miniature world mirrors the dreams and wishes of little girls and their society. As if in a time warp, collectors can go back and relive the early 1960s with Barbie in her outfit á la Jackie Kennedy, bubble cut hairdo in her typical American dream home. Or isn't it fun to again see "Beatle" Ken and Barbie in her miniskirt ready for Woodstock? Girls growing up in the 1960s played with a fashion shop, a school, and a little theater. Twenty years later modern times replaced these with a fitness center, an office, and a rock stage.

It is fascinating to see how Barbie dolls from other countries reflect the ideals of foreign societies. Barbie dolls sold in Japan in the 1980s have round blue eyes, blond hair, and a delicate figure. Barbie dolls from Brazil look as wild and sexy as any participant of the Rio Carnival. In Greece little girls were given Barbie dolls strapped to a candle to be held in religious processions.

Over the years thousands of different Barbie dolls, and even more outfits, were sold all over the world. The first part of this book shows a complete line of Barbie and her family that were available in the United States from the beginning in 1959 to 1989. Also pictured are all Barbie dolls sold in Germany at that time (and Barbie doll's predecessor Lilli) as well as many other foreign dolls.

The second part of the book deals with foreign outfits, cases, displays, and outfit variations, in short: unusual items that haven't been published before. Not all Barbie dolls available in the U.S. were offered in Europe. In the first years (Barbie dolls were sold there from 1963 on) nearly all dolls and outfits were sold in regular (English language) boxes, even special dolls sold only in Germany. From 1978 on European and Canadian dolls came in multilingual boxes. This book shows many regular U.S. dolls in foreign boxes. If not specifically mentioned this different packaging doesn't make a big price difference. Some Barbie dolls are made by other companies under license from Mattel. This way is chosen when duty barriers make it difficult or impossible to import regular Barbie dolls.

Often the dolls were offered at different times in different countries. This book pictures the items under the first year that they

were sold anywhere. Not shown are some of the Barbie dolls that are basically the same dolls as offered before but have minor changes in painting,
hand molding, or outfit.

Barbie dolls available in different hair colors are shown only in one hair
tone if there is no big price difference between the colors.

There are two prices given in this book. The first is for items in complete
and mint condition. The second price is for dolls that are "Never
Removed from Box" — NRFB*. Good condition dolls are worth about
half to two thirds of the mint doll price. Dolls that were played with
a lot and/or have obvious problems like cut hair or missing fingers fetch only a quarter or less of the mint price.

The prices given here should only be used as a guideline. Prices
vary from dealer to dealer, coast to coast and often follow the gen-
eral economy. The market for Barbie dolls is based — like every
other market — on the law of supply and demand. A large ware-
house find can bring the price of a particular doll down (at least in
a short run). New waves of collec-tors and the rising popularity of this hobby on the other hand, often catapult prices to unknown heights. At the moment there is no end of the Barbie collector boom in sight. Every little girl (or boy) now playing with Barbie dolls is a potential new collector in a few years.

*At least 20% of the value is
taken off this price once
the item has been removed
from the original package
(= MIB, Mint in Box).

Prices for Barbie dolls from the mid 1970s are still relatively low. Also Ken dolls and most of his outfits are not high in demand now. This could change soon. There are more and more new male collectors who often favor Ken. And the generation who played with Barbie dolls in the 1970s is now ready and able to invest greater sums into the dolls of their childhood.

The most valuable part of nearly all outfits is the little accessories that were easily lost (like jewelry, paper items, gloves, shoes). The outfit by itself, all accessories missing, may be worth only one third or even one tenth of the complete outfit. The prices given are for mint and complete outfits (not including the price of the modelling doll).

Happy hunting!

Shown on page 5:
◆ **Ken A Go Go, #1432, 1966, $400.00.**
◆ **American Girl Barbie modeling lamé sheath, pak, 1963, $90.00.**
Shown opposite:
◆ **Redheaded Twist Barbie in Scene Stealers, #1845, 1966, $180.00.**
◆ **Lilli unpacking early 1950s (pre-Barbie) Mattel doll furniture, furniture each $50.00/$30.00.**
Shown at right:
◆ **Ken in Here Comes the Groom, #1426, 1966, $700.00. American Girl Barbie wearing Here Comes the Bride, #1665, 1965, $350.00.**

Barbie Through the Years

The Beginning, Lilli

Barbie is a German "Fräuleinwunder." Her history started in this country some years after the end of World War II. A famous West German newsletter, *Bild*, asked Reinhard Beuthin, one of their cartoonists, to fill a gap in the newsletter issue of June 24, 1952. His cartoon, featuring Lilli, a sexy young lady who plays with her admirers, became a regular institution. Lilli was so popular that *Bild* decided to make a doll out of this character.

The Lilli doll was created by Max Weissbrodt from the famous Hausser/Elastolin company in Neustadt/Coburg, Germany. Martah Maar, the mother of the company's owner (Rolf Hausser), ran a large and well-known doll company, "3 M Dolls." In this factory Lillis were put together and dressed.

August 12, 1955, was the first day Lilli dolls were sold in Germany. They were offered mostly in smoke shops, with a few toy shops carrying them. Later some of these dolls found their way to other countries; they were even sold in the U. S. Lillis made for export came on doll stands that have only "Lilli" written on them, while the regular dolls stands say "Bild-Lilli."

- Poplin dress, no. 1109.
- Lilli cartoon book, $230.00.
- Newspaper that accompanied most Lillis, $100.00.
- Stand for small Lilli, $180.00.
- Stand for large Lilli, $250.00.

These stands work the same way as the first Barbie stand later did. Out of a round base comes a metal wire that fits into a hole in the doll's feet (shoes).

Lilli's original package consisted of the stand as bottom and a clear plastic cylinder and a removable lid out of the same material.

Each doll was accompanied by a beautiful and funny miniature version of a *Bild* newspaper.

Lilli dolls are not marked. They were sold in two different sizes, 7" and 11½". Her black shoes and earrings were molded on and not removable. A few dolls with brown shoes have been found. A Lilli with painted on long brown boots and a garter is the only one known of its kind. Lilli's face, her earrings, shoes, and fingernails were hand painted. Nearly all dolls have blonde hair. Only a few were made as special orders with brunette or red hair.

♦ **Nurse, no. 1143.**
♦ **Skirt with blouse, no. 1121.**
♦ **Dress with jacket.**

♦ **Boucle skirt with evening pull-over and silver jewelry, no. 1182.**
♦ **Stewardess (missing hat).**

The inside doll construction is like that of earlier baby dolls. The limbs are fastened by fabric coated rubber bands. These are often quite tight and cause the hard plastic of the body to crack. Most Lillis have this problem, even never removed from box dolls. It doesn't subtract much from the doll's value and can be repaired. The hair is not sewn into the head, it is fastened between the face and a separate back part. A big metallic screw (hidden under the finished hairdo) holds the two parts together. Lilli is a beauty with her spitcurl and ponytail. But her hairdo was meant to be looked at, not to be played with. To make her ponytail not look so voluminous about one third of the hair was cut shorter. Only when you open the ponytail do you notice the different lengths of hair.

The doll was quite expensive then (19, 90 German marks for a large Lilli), about four times the price Americans had to pay for the first Barbie dolls a few years later. The original target group was adults. She was planned as a promotional article and a joke for adults, but Lilli's biggest success was as a toy. Children were crazy about her. So her outfits, that were available separately, became more modest than they had been. Lilli's dresses are easily identified by the sort of press button used. They consist of two parts that are pressed from the inside and the outside into the garment. The outside of the outfit shows a round metal press button painted in a color matching the garment. There is a little hole in the middle of nearly all the buttons. Only the ones that could be seen in front of the outfit are missing it. Inside the buttons are marked "PRYM."

Some accessories were available for Lilli. They were not sold in large numbers and are even harder to come by today than the dolls. Her chair in the typical 1950s style has a wire frame covered with plastic. Lilli's poodle is a mystery. Dogs found together with the doll are Steiff poodles. It is common practice for companies that need accessories, to buy them from other companies and then sell them together with their goods. The Steiff dog, that is the right size, may have become Lilli's dog this way.

There is a Lilli shop display that is the only one of its kind so far. Made out of unfinished wood, the gymnast rings and a ladder have a single wire protruding from a plywood base, which is inserted into the foot of a 7" Lilli doll. Both the red enamel bench and black table with white laminated paper top are made out of wood. Originally these four items came on a square of unfinished plywood.

NRFB = Never removed from box.	
Prices: **NRFB large Lillis**	**$2500**
Mint large Lillis nude	**$1200**
Played with large Lillis nude	**$700**
NRFB small Lillis	**$1300**
Mint small Lillis nude	**$500**
Played with small Lillis nude	**$350**
Outfits: regular (pants, shirt)	**$350**
for small Lilli	**$250**
dresses or unusual	**$450+**
for small Lilli	**$350+**
For a different hair color add	**$600.00**

It is unknown to many collectors, but in the 1960s, Reinhard Beuthin (Lilli's spiritual father) working at that time for the Munich *Abendzeitung* paper created another cartoon character who later was also transformed into a doll, Schwabienchen. This doll, one may say a sister of Barbie, was produced by the "3 M" doll company. Previously, this company had put together and dressed Lilli dolls. Schwabienchen is a little bit smaller than Lilli or Barbie and not very appealing to collectors. Most interesting are her outfits. Some of them are left over Lilli dresses that were shortened a little because of the difference in size.

Lillis were very popular so other companies quickly came out with similar dolls. These copies are easily identified by the lack of quality and style and also the mark "Hong Kong" on their backs. These "Hong Kong Lillis," as they are called, were sold in different sizes and are still easily found today.

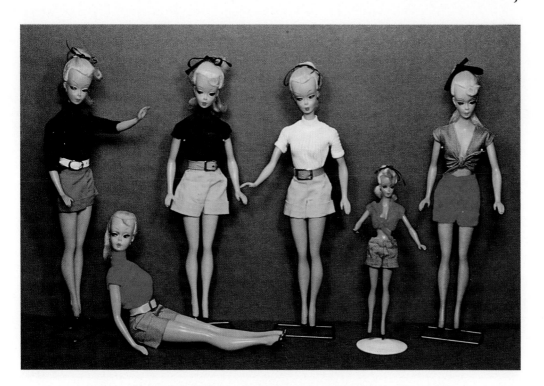

◆ **Four Lillis in shorts, a pullover, and belt, no. 1113.**
◆ **Two Lillis in shorts and wrap shirt, no. 1119.**

◆ **Two Lillis in ¾ length pants with belt, no 1117.**
◆ **Long pants, bra, and straw hat, no. 1115.**
◆ **¾ length pants with belt, no. 1117.**
◆ **Home outfit and a variation top, no. 1139.**
◆ **¾ length pants with beach shirt, no. 1118.**

The
Beginning,
Lilli

♦ Bikini with jacket, no. 1179 (?).
♦ Beach suit, no. 1166.
♦ Bikini with beach hat, no. 1142.
♦ Bathing suit with beach jacket no. 1172.
♦ Three Lillis in bathing suits with beach jackets, no. 1134.

♦ Two Lillis in beach dresses with shorts, no. 1164.
♦ Summer dress with flowers, no. 1123.
♦ Bathing suit with beach jacket, no. 1172.

- **Four Lillis in shorty pajamas, no. 1155.**
- **Two Lillis in pajamas, no. 1144.**
- **Two Lillis in dressing gowns, no. 1162.**

- **Ballerina, no. 1131.**   - **Four skaters, no. 1141.**

♦ **Dirndl with pockets, no. 1176.**
♦ **Dirndl, no. 1178.**
♦ **Lilli chair, no. 101, $300.00.**
♦ **Two Lillis in tennis dresses with rackets, no. 1154.**

♦ **All five Lillis in dirndl, no. 1120. The little crochet bag came with only
a few of these outfits.**

- ◆ **Dirndl, no. 1178.**
- ◆ **Skirt with edging and pullover, no. 1153.**
- ◆ **Hula girl, no. 1136.**
- ◆ **Dirndl with black bodice, no. 1175.**
- ◆ **Two Lillis dressed as Hungarian girls, no. 1140.**

- ◆ **Three Lillis wearing a velvet ensemble with blouse, no. 1130.**
- ◆ **Cocktail dress, no. 1133 (?)**
- ◆ **Floating Lilli, a special edition sold with a magic kit by H.G. Patsch.**
- ◆ **Prototype outfit.**

The
Beginning,
Lilli

◆ **Evening gown, no. 1122.**
◆ **Cocktail dress, no. 1157 (special edition Lilli, note the painted boots).**
◆ **Two Lillis dressed in a ballgown with net lace, no. 1124.**

◆ **Cocktail dress, no. 1156.**
◆ **Cocktail dress, no. 1150.**
◆ **Dress with velvet belt, no. 1170.**
◆ **Gold Lamé evening gown, no. 1105.**
◆ **Ballgown, no. 1171.**

- ◆ Coat, no. 1177.
- ◆ Ocelot jacket with ¾ length pants, no. 1183.
- ◆ Lilli's dog, $200.00.
- ◆ Two Lillis wearing ¾ length pants with fur jacket, no. 1151.

- ◆ Home outfit with stockinet top, no. 1159.
- ◆ Apre's ski, no. 1161.
- ◆ Denim outfit, no. 1145.
- ◆ Three Lillis wearing anoraks with ¾ length pants and pullovers, no. 1129.

The
Beginning,
Lilli

- Prototype outfit.
- Colored long pants, pullover, and scarf, no. 1160.
- Colored long pants, pullover, and jacket.
- Two dolls in Norwegian anoraks with hoods and long pants, no. 1148. Pants worn by the large Lilli have been shortened. Note the eyeglasses!
- Dufflecoat, no. 1167.

- All three Lillis in poplin jackets and shorts, no. 1117.
- Swing, no. 100/30, $150.00.
- Lilli's dog, $200.00.

The Beginning, Lilli

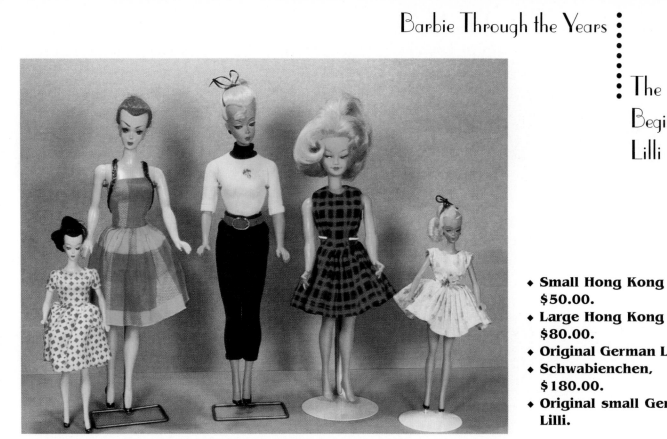

- ◆ **Small Hong Kong Lilli, $50.00.**
- ◆ **Large Hong Kong Lilli, $80.00.**
- ◆ **Original German Lilli.**
- ◆ **Schwabienchen, $180.00.**
- ◆ **Original small German Lilli.**

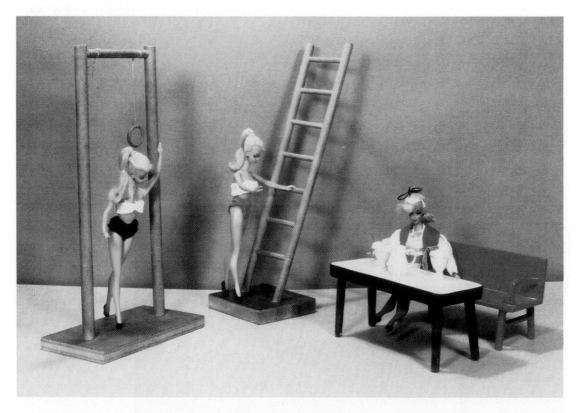

◆ **Lilli display (jar and cups are a later addition), priced without dolls, $2,000.00.**

The
Beginning,
Lilli

- ◆ Large Hong Kong Lilli with red hair, $100.00.
- ◆ Large Kong Kong Lilli, mint in package (MIP), $200.00.
- ◆ Two small Hong Kong Lillis, $50.00 each.
- ◆ Small Hong Kong Lilli, mint in box (MIB), $120.00.
- ◆ Large MIB Hong Kong Lilli (MIB), $180.00.

◆ No. 1 Barbie and Lilli.

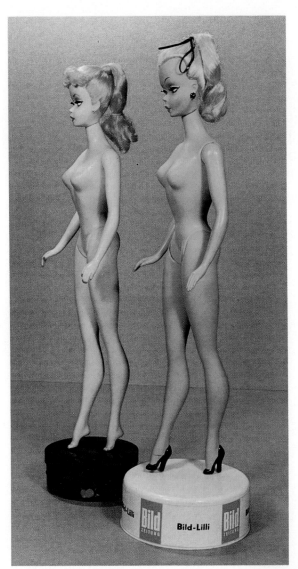

◆ **Lilli and No. 1 Barbie.**

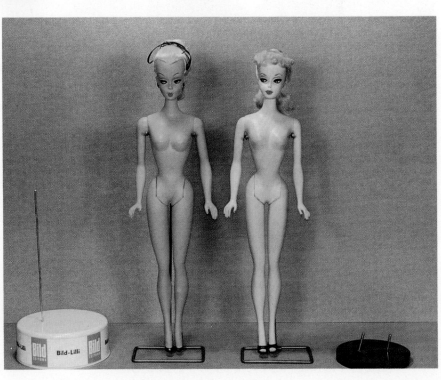

1959

While traveling in Europe, Ruth Handler, co-owner and founder of Mattel, saw a Lilli doll in a toy shop in Lucerne, Switzerland. This was the doll she was looking for. Mrs. Handler wanted to produce a doll with adult proportions since she noticed that her own daughter Barbie (after whom the doll was later named) loved playing with paper dolls with adult features, not with baby dolls. So Ruth Handler bought some of these dolls and took them home to show them to the development department of Mattel. Here Lilli underwent some changes. Her body construction was altered, the elastic inside removed. The body became solid and the head was held on by a neck knob. Shoes and earrings were now removable. The hairdo changed a little, too. The spitcurl became full bangs. The eyes stayed black and white, but the new eyebrows were more pointed. Lilli's face was handpainted, Barbie doll's features were printed on.

Except for these small changes Barbie is identical to a large Lilli in size and appearance. Even the type of stand used was the same. The legs of large Lillis are hollow, so one long wire inserted into the dolls feet and legs could hold Lilli safely. But this wire could be a danger to children. Barbie doll's legs are solid, allowing only a short wire to be inserted. This could not hold the weight of the doll, so a stand with wires for both feet was created for the first Barbie. To insure a good fit two metal cylinders were inserted into the holes in her feet. Barbie came in two hair colors, blonde, and the harder-to-find brunette. The plastic material used for the first three types of Barbie dolls fades easily. Most of these dolls are now ivory colored.

Mattel bought the worldwide patent rights for the Lilli doll and stand from the *Bild* newspaper.

◆ **Brunette No. 1 Barbie, $3,500.00, wearing Easter Parade, #971, 1959, $1,200.00.**

Barbie had her debut at the New York Toy Fair in February of 1959. At first the buyers weren't particularly excited about this new doll that was so different from the popular baby dolls. But the first series of 500,000 Barbie dolls and a million outfits (all produced in Japan) sold out quickly. Mattel marketed Barbie very intelligently. They introduced Barbie on TV during the popular *Mickey Mouse Club.* The doll was promoted also on Viewmaster disks. Shop displays were set up at counters with dressed dolls to show how the outfits would look on a doll.

At the end of 1959 the second type of Barbie came on the market. The only difference from the first Barbie was that she no longer had the holes and metal cylinders in her feet.

♦ **No. 2 Barbie, brunette with braided hairdo, $2,800.00/$3,900.00.**

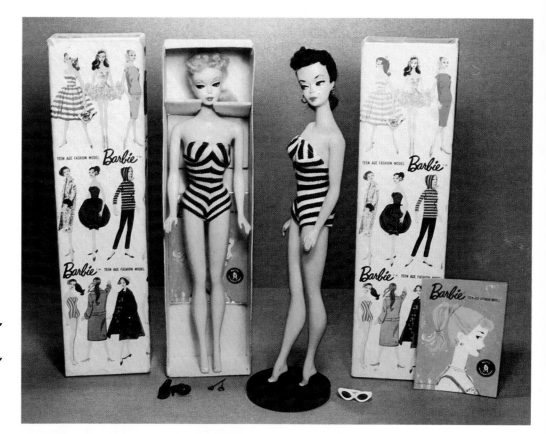

- **Blonde No. 1 Barbie,**
  $3,000.00/$3,700.00.
- **Brunette, No. 1 Barbie,**
  $3,500.00/$4,000.00.

- **No. 2 Barbie, brunette, $2,300.00/$3,400.00 (add $500.00 for rare braided hairstyle).**
- **No. 2 Barbie blonde, $2,000.00/$3,000.00.**

24 •••

1960

1960 marked the introduction of the third Barbie. She has blue irises and curved eyebrows. Some No. 3 Barbie dolls came with brown eyeliner, some with blue.

The boxes of the first Barbie type are marked with a little TM. From late 1959 on boxes show an ® instead. In Canada Barbie was offered first in the 1959 Sears Christmas catalog, but the earliest Barbie found in Canada by collectors is a No. 3 doll (surprisingly in a TM marked box). The fourth Barbie is identical in looks but is made of a different type of plastic that didn't fade.

Collectors often find transitional dolls that show the fading only on some part of the body.

- **No. 2 blonde Barbie, modeling a rare pink Sweet Dreams #973, 1959, $300.00.**
- **Brunette No. 3 Barbie with unusual curved eyebrows (perhaps a prototype), $800.00 in Sweet Dreams #973, 1959, $50.00.**
- **Suzy Goose vanity, $60.00.**

1960

- **No. 3 Barbie, brunette, $500.00/$800.00.**
- **No. 3 Barbie, blonde, $400.00/$700.00.**
- **Transitional Barbie, $300.00/$600.00.**

- **No. 4 Barbie, blonde, $300.00/$550.00.**
- **No. 4 Barbie, brunette, $350.00/$600.00.**

1961

This year's big news is Ken. He is Barbie doll's new boyfriend, named after the Handlers' son. The first version of this doll has flocked hair that easily rubs off. He was available with blond, black, or as a department store special with brown hair.

Barbie doll's new body is hollow. She now also comes with red hair. The very popular Bubble Cut hair style is introduced. A greasy shine was caused by chemical reactions in the plastic material of some doll heads from this year (this does not subtract from the doll's value).

Most Barbie dolls from this year have bright red lips.

- **First Ken and Barbie in Registered Nurse, #991, 1961, $120.00.**
- **Go Together furniture and background.**

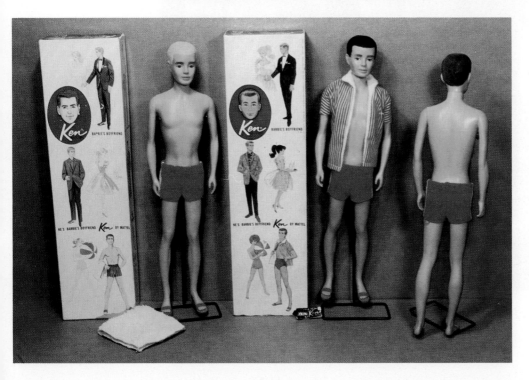

- **First Ken (with flocked blond or black hair), $100.00/$180.00.**
- **First Ken with brown hair, $200.00/$300.00.**

◆ **Three Bubble Cut Barbie dolls with greasy faces, $130.00/$270.00 each.**

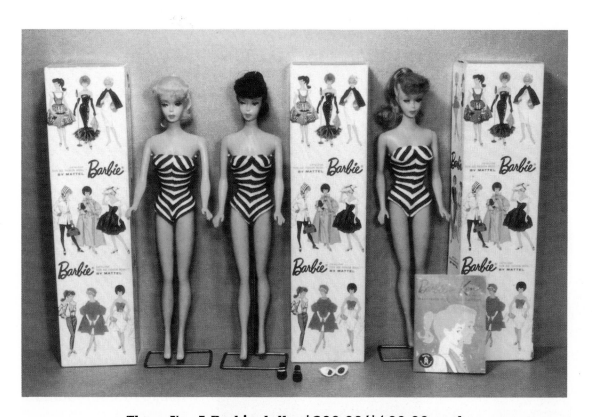

◆ **Three No. 5 Barbie dolls, $200.00/$400.00 each.**

1962

Ken gets a new head mold. His hair is no longer flocked on but painted in blond or brunet.

Barbie looks a little bit more innocent in her re-designed red bathing suit. Her lip color varies from bright red to pink. Her new box doesn't show the Gay Parisienne outfit on the cover anymore.

◆ **Ponytail and Bubble Cut Barbie dolls with their companions in Suzy Goose boats. Blue boat $200.00, green boat $150.00. Ken is wearing the yachtsman outfit with rare hat, #789, 1964, $280.00.**

* **Three Ken dolls with painted hair (No. 2 Ken): standing, $60.00/$120.00; sitting Ken with a pale head (may be made from No. 1 Barbie material), $150.00/$250.00.**
* **Three No. 6 Ponytail Barbie dolls, $180.00/$400.00 each.**

* **Four Bubble Cut Barbie dolls, $120.00/$250.00 each.**

1963

Barbie gets her first girlfriend, Midge. This doll was very popular and is still relatively easy to find today. However, two rare variations are highly sought after by collectors: Midge with teeth and Midge without freckles.

Midge and Barbie dolls now come on bodies that are marked with both their names, called Midge/Barbie bodies. Earlier dolls had bodies marked Barbie.

Fashion Queen Barbie is the first doll with a molded hairdo. Her three interchangeable wigs match all of her outfits.

The new Ken is quite unusual. Last year's head comes on a ¼" shorter body. The kneecaps are more pronounced, the feet fleshier. The cutest new doll is a baby from "Barbie Baby-Sits" (No. 953).

◆ **Ken in Play Ball #792, 1963, $50.00, in front of the Barbie College.**

1963

♦ **Standing: Three Midge dolls, each $60.00/$180.00.**
♦ **Sitting: Midge with teeth, $170.00/$450.00; Midge without freckles, $200.00/$450.00.**

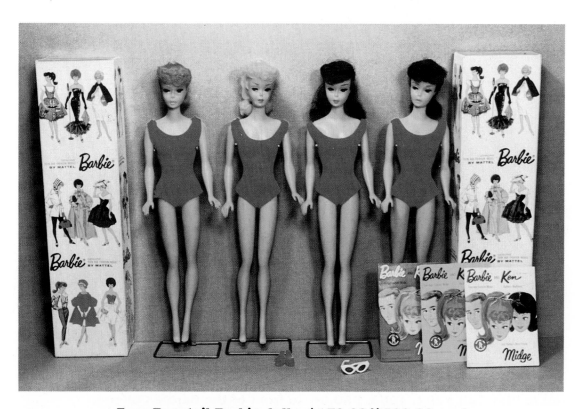

♦ **Four Ponytail Barbie dolls, $170.00/$300.00 each.**

◆ **Eleven Bubble Cut Barbie dolls, $100.00/$200.00 each.**

◆ **Fashion Queen Barbie, $100.00/$450.00.**
◆ **Shorter version Ken with painted hair, $80.00/$200.00.**
◆ **Barbie Baby Sits set, No. 953 (pictured with a Fashion Queen Barbie),**
  $120.00/$300.00.

1964

This was the first year Barbie had bendable legs (knees). The first doll having this mobility, Miss Barbie with sleep-eyes, wasn't a big success because of her hard plastic face. These dolls in good condition are now highly priced collectibles. Over the time the hard plastic of her face reacts with the plastic softener in her interchangeable wigs that children left on the doll, so most of these dolls show a lot of meltmarks. Miss Barbie doll's neck knob is smaller than any other because of the room needed for the sleep-eye weights. Barbie doll's Wig Wardrobe consists of the head and wigs of Fashion Queen Barbie. This year's Ken has the same height as the 1962 model.

Two new characters enter the world of Barbie: Skipper, Barbie doll's little sister and Allan, a boyfriend for Midge. He is the same size as Ken. His striped beach jacket comes in two variations,

◆ **Skipper in Me 'N My Doll, #1913, 1965, $90.00; an unusual Miss Barbie with unpainted hair, $550.00, in Dancing Doll, #1626, 1965, $160.00.**

◆ **Miss Barbie with an unpainted head, $550.00.**

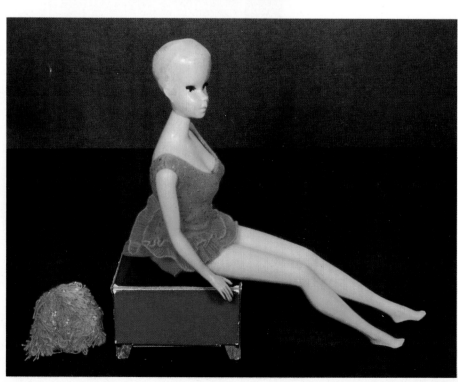

◆ **Miss Barbie, $450.00/$1,500.00.**

vertical stripes are much harder to find. Skipper doll's metallic hair band can cause her skin and hair to discolor. It's the same chemical process that causes Barbie doll's ears to turn green around metallic earrings. It is best to remove these metallic objects from the dolls. Collectors are still looking for the best remedies against the discolorations. Another very popular doll with collectors is Swirl Ponytail Barbie. She comes in the same red bathing suit as the Bubble Cut dolls.

Barbie now is also available in Europe. The brunette Swirl Ponytail Barbie dolls sold in Europe, as well as brunette Bubble Cut Barbie dolls sold in Europe and in Canada, are dressed in Fashion Queen (white and gold striped) bathing suits and come with white No. 1 shoes with holes in their bottoms (regular shoes in Canada).

For the first few years Barbie dolls in Germany were distributed by the famous Schildkroet (Turtle Mark) company. Barbie and her outfits were quite expensive in Europe and only a small percentage of little girls were lucky enough to own one.

◆ **Four Swirl Ponytail Barbie dolls, $260.00/ $500.00 each.**
◆ **Swirl Ponytail Barbie from Germany, $350.00/$650.00.**
◆ **Bubble Cut Barbie sold in Canada and Germany, $250.00/ $400.00.**

◆ Seven First Skipper dolls, $60.00/$120.00 each, add up to $50.00 for an unusual haircolor (as all dolls that are not shown in their original boxes have).

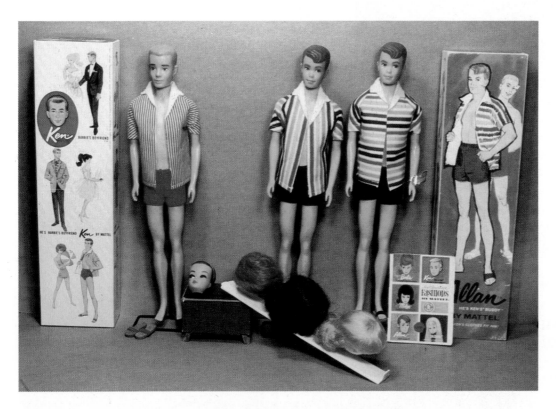

◆ Ken with painted hair, $60.00/$120.00.
◆ Barbie Wig Wardrobe, $60.00/$300.00.
◆ Allan, $80.00/$180.00.
◆ Allan with variation jacket, $110.00/$240.00.

1965

Barbie, Midge, Ken, Allan, and Skipper are now all available with "lifelike" bendable legs. Today Bendable Leg Barbie with her new hairdo and light orange lips is especially popular, her price doubling every few years. Bendable Leg Ken comes with or without blush and in a rare version with a greasy face.

A favorite of many collectors is an unusual Bubble Cut Barbie with a sidepart hairdo (called Sidepart Bubble Cut Barbie).

A Midge head with molded hair is sold with three unique wigs (Midge doll's Wig Wardrobe). This head is also available together with a Fashion Queen head in a Color 'N Curl set (a similar set was offered with one Barbie head only). Some of these heads were found a few years ago in old doll clinics. A few of these have a lot of blush and a more vivid face coloring.

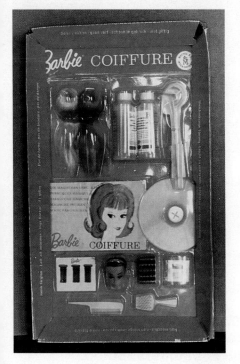

◆ **Color 'N Curl Set (Coiffure), European box marked 1966, $150.00/ $350.00.**

Skipper gets two new friends: Skooter and Ricky. They all share the same body mold.

The Barbie Baby Sits Set now comes with a few new accessories.

Some of the Skipper dolls sold in Japan are very unusual. Instead of blue irises they have eyes painted only in black and white. They were sold as dressed dolls.

- ◆ **Bendable Leg Midge, $330.00/$550.00.**
- ◆ **Skooter (blonde and brunette) in School Days, #1907, 1964, $50.00.**
- ◆ **Three Molded Hair Midge dolls (Wig Wardrobe), $200.00/$500.00 each modeling:**
    - ◆ **Sweater Girl (orange/gray), #976, 1959, $50.00;**
    - ◆ **Knitting Pretty (pink), #957, 1964, $200.00;**
    - ◆ **Knitting Pretty (blue), #957, 1963, $70.00.**
- ◆ **Extra heads and hair accessories: Color 'N Curl Set, $250.00/$450.00.**

1965

◆ **Bendable Leg Allan, $200.00/$550.00.**
◆ **Bendable Leg Ken, $150.00/$280.00.**
◆ **Bendable Leg (American Girl) Barbie, $380.00/$750.00.**

◆ **Ricky, $70.00/$160.00.**
◆ **Skooter, $60.00/$140.00.**
◆ **Japanese Skipper, $350.00/$500.00.**
◆ **Bendable Leg Skipper, $90.00/$270.00.**

- Bubble Cut Barbie in a homemade outfit out of Barbie material, $100.00 (for the dress).
- Barbie Baby Sits set second version, #953, $170.00/$350.00.
- Bendable Leg Ken with greasy face, $280.00/$550.00, wearing Sailor, #796, 1963, $50.00.

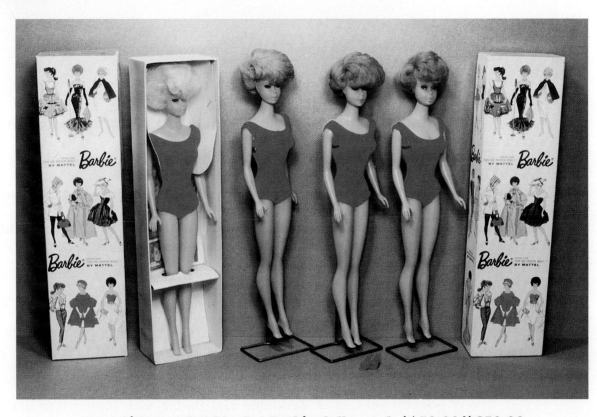

- Four Sidepart Bubble Cut Barbie dolls, each $450.00/$650.00.

1966

1966 is one of the most interesting and confusing years for collectors. Several types of dolls emerged out of last year's Bendable Leg (B/L) Barbie. The most sought after, Sidepart Barbie, has an elaborate hairstyle. The hair is longer and not parted in the middle but on the side. The rarest B/L Barbie with a sidepart hairdo comes from Japan. Her skin tone is pinker than the American ver-

- **European American Girl Barbie with pink skin tone, $2,500.00/$4,000.00, in Benefit Performance, #1667, 1966, $480.00.**
- **Japanese Sidepart American Girl Barbie, $3,700.00/$5,000.00, modeling a rare Japanese Kimono, $700.00.**
- **Sidepart American Girl Barbie, $2,500.00/$3,500.00, showing Gala Abend, German exclusive, #1677, 1967, $600.00.**
- **European/Japanese pink skin tone Bubble Cut Barbie, $1,000.00/$1,500.00, in Campus Sweetheart, #1616, 1965, $450.00 and a prototype fur jacket, $500.00.**

sion. The Japanese sidepart Barbie was also sold with a straight leg body. Buyers of Sidepart Barbie dolls should be aware of many fakes. Often other Barbie heads are re-rooted and offered as original Sideparts. Original Sidepart Barbie doll's hairline is not "V" shaped in front of the ear, while the hairline of fakes have to fill out the holes left over from the original hairdo.

A very popular version of Bendable Leg Barbie with longer hair and a more vivid make up is not easy to find. Collectors call her "High Color B/L Barbie."

A few B/L Barbie dolls were found with Swirl Ponytail Barbie heads, their boxes are marked "Ponytail." Also hard to find are Bendable Leg Barbie dolls with a Bubble Cut head and a sidepart hairdo.

In Europe and Japan Barbie dolls with this hairdo, straight legs, and a very pink skin tone were sold in small numbers, as were pink skin High Color B/L Barbie dolls that came on standard bodies.

At the end of the year a very unusual B/L Barbie was sold in Germany. She comes on a regular Bendable Leg body that also has the unusual pink skin tone. Her head is about the same as next years standard Barbie, only it looks a little bit wider. She comes in many different haircolors. The hair material used is very coarse. Her box is the same as one of the regular Bendable Leg Barbie doll's, only a little sticker on the top of the box that tells her new stock number (#1163).

Color Magic Barbie also comes on a Bendable Leg body. Her hair and costume are color changeable. She was offered in two hair colors; very rare Midnight Black that changes to Ruby Red and more common Golden Blonde which becomes Scarlet Flame. Most of these dolls have very vivid make-up, a few have been found with the older style of make-up (smaller lips in pastel colors that often fade).

In Japan Midge doll's freckled face was not appealing to their ideal of beauty and so a special Midge without freckles and with a different head mold was produced for this market, a rarity today.

Finally Skooter got bendable legs, too. The first issues of B/L Skipper and Skooter still have the old grayish skintone, the second issue of these dolls produced later in the year have a pink skin tone. The earliest type of Skipper and Skooter dolls with straight legs (as well, as Ricky) were offered this year with this new skin tone.

◆ **Japanese Sidepart American Girl Barbie, $3,700.00/ $5,000.00 modeling a rare Japanese kimono, $700.00.**
◆ **Japanese Midge with molded hair, $2,000.00/ $3,000.00, wearing another Japanese kimono (replaced obi), #B 901-1, $600.00.**

1966

Francie, Barbie doll's cousin, one of many collector's favorite characters, was introduced this year. She is 11¼" tall and the first doll that was offered with real eyelashes. She comes with bendable or straight legs (this version has only painted lashes contrary to the description on her box). Some of the brunette Francies sold in Japan have blue eyes (instead of the usual brown), red lips, a pink skin tone, and lashes, even in the straight leg version. As the Japanese Midge and Skipper, Francie was available in Japan as an already dressed doll.

Two other new additions to the Barbie family are Barbie doll's twin siblings, Tutti and Todd. They were sold by themselves as well as in four different play-sets (that came in a few variations): Walkin' My Dolly, Night-Night Sleep Tight, Me and My Dog, and Melody in Pink. Tutti looks so cute with her blonde or brunette hair; in the play-set Night-Night Sleep Tight she even has red hair. Todd is red headed. A rarity is a brunet Todd from this year (brunet Todds with smaller heads were sold from 1975 to 1980 in Europe).

- **Color Magic Barbie dolls: red or black hair $900.00/$1,500.00, blonde $500.00/ $1,200.00, with coral lips $550.00/$1,300.00.**
- **Bendable Leg Skooter, $80.00/$250.00.**

- ◆ German American Girl Barbie, #1163, $900.00/$1,800.00.
- ◆ American Girl Barbie with high color face, $800.00/$1,200.00.
- ◆ American Girl Barbie with Swirl Ponytail head, $700.00/$1,000.00.
- ◆ American Girl Barbie with Bubble Cut Sidepart head, $900.00/ $1,300.00.
- ◆ Box stamped on top: Blond Pony, belongs to Swirl Ponytail American Girl Barbie. Box on the bottom with sticker 1163 came with the German American Girl Barbie.

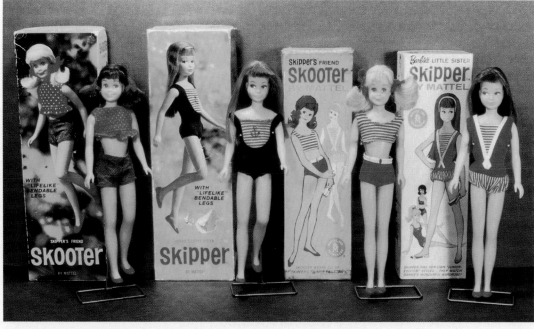

- ◆ Pink Skin Bendable Leg Skooter, $90.00/$300.00.
- ◆ Pink Skin Bendable Leg Skipper, $90.00/$300.00.
- ◆ Pink Skin Straight Leg Skooter, $70.00/$150.00, or Skipper, $70.00/$180.00.

- ◆ Bendable Leg Francie, $110.00/$300.00.
- ◆ Straight Leg Francie (brunette or blonde), (notice the different swim suit bottoms), $150.00/$250.00 each.
- ◆ Straight Leg Francie from Japan, sold in outfit #211102210, $700.00/$1,000.00.

- ◆ Tutti, $50.00/$100.00.
- ◆ Me and My Dog Tutti set, $180.00/$300.00.
- ◆ Pink Skin Ricky, $80.00/$170.00.
- ◆ Todd with brown hair found in Germany, $400.00/$500.00, wearing the coat of the German outfit Mein neuer Mantel, #8598, 1973, $50.00.
- ◆ Todd, $60.00/$150.00.

44 ●●●

- ◆ **Three Melody in Pink Tutti dolls, $160.00/$280.00 each.**
- ◆ **Three Night-Night Sleep Tight dolls, the regular edition shown on top $90.00/$180.00, the rare versions on the bottom, each $130.00/ $250.00.**
- ◆ **Two Walkin' My Dolly sets, common version on top, $125.00/$250.00; hard-to-find version on bottom, $180.00/$300.00.**

- ◆ **Tutti and Todd Sundae Treat, $180.00/$350.00 (notice the furniture in two different shades of pink).**

1967

To keep up with changing styles Barbie gets a face lift. Her heavy plastic lashes are replaced by rooted eyelashes, her hair following the latest fashion becomes long and straight, she looks ten years younger and more innocent. But not only her face, her body changes, too. With her new Twist 'N Turn waist she is more poseable than ever before. The new Twist 'N Turn (TNT) Barbie was offered in a big trade-in promotion for $1.50 plus an old Barbie. Imagine how many No. 1 and No. 2 Barbie dolls were traded in and given to charity.

This new head mold is also used for the Barbie Hair Fair Set, a Barbie head with interchangeable hair pieces and accessories, and for a Standard Barbie. This doll doesn't have lashes, a twist waist, nor bendable legs. Her eyes look to the side and she comes on the same type of body with the same markings as the last Bubble Cut Barbie dolls, but a pink skin tone.

Francie, now also available in a Twist version, gets two new friends: Casey and the personality doll Twiggy (who looks like a blonde Casey except for her shorter hair and heavier make-up. The rarest of all Francie dolls is a black version of this doll (Black Francie).

Tutti is offered in two new playsets: Cookin' Goodies and Swing-A-Ling. She gets a new outfit, and most important a new friend, Chris.

Pink skin straight leg Skipper and Skooter, as well as a Swirl Ponytail Barbie in a Fashion Queen swim suit, are sold in small numbers in a special (and now hard to find) doll case.

- ◆ **Skipper and Skooter case, #2001/2002, with doll, $200.00.**

- ◆ **Hair Fair head (on a body), $60.00/$200.00, wearing Underliners, #1821, 1968, $50.00.**
- ◆ **Mod A Go Go Suzy Goose Francie bed (coat hanger not pictured), rare, $700.00.**

- Twiggy, $150.00/$330.00.
- Casey, $130.00/$290.00.
- Twist Francie, $140.00/$350.00.
- Standard Barbie, $180.00/ $400.00.
- Twist Barbie, $150.00/$320.00.

- Chris, $80.00/$180.00.
- Swing A Ling Tutti set (head band not pictured), $160.00/$270.00.
- Two Cookin' Goodies (aprons missing), $150.00/$240.00.
- Tutti, $50.00/$100.00.
- Background: Barbie and Skipper Schoolroom.

1968

Barbie and her friends can talk! Just pull the string in the back and they say different sentences. Most of these talking dolls are mute today because of deteriorating rubber bands inside, but they can be repaired to talk again. Another problem with these dolls (and many following doll types up to the mid 1970s) are limbs that fall off or melt into the body. That is caused by the softener in the plastic of the limbs that reacts with the hard plastic fixtures of the body. Most of the talking Barbie dolls speak English, a few Spanish. In Europe Barbie and her friends spoke French and German, also Japanese talking Barbie dolls are known. Barbie doll's new friend Stacey speaks with a British accent. Talking Christie was made from the Midge head mold.

All dolls up to this year were manufactured in Japan. From 1968 on, production was moved to other countries with cheaper labor costs like Mexico, Korea, The Philippines, and Taiwan. Every Barbie shows the country of production in her marking. This gives a good hint to identify the age of an unknown Barbie (the year date in the marking doesn't show the year of production or selling, but the date the body form was copyrighted). The same body forms are often used for decades.

Twist N' Turn Barbie gets a new swim suit (with an unusual and now hard-to-find belt). Stacey and Skooter are also offered in a Twist version. The cutest new addition of 1968 is a Tutti size personality doll, Buffy with her doll Mrs. Beasley, based on the characters from the popular "Family Affair" television show. She comes with reddish or blonde hair.

- ◆ **Two Buffy and Mrs. Beasley sets, blonde and reddish hair, $100.00/$200.00 ea.**
- ◆ **Tutti wearing the European outfit Ich geh spazieren, #8591, 1974, dress, $35.00.**
- ◆ **Tutti and Todd Dutch Bedroom Furniture set by Suzy Goose, rare, $900.00.**
- ◆ **Background Skipper Dream Room.**

- ◆ **Talking Barbie, $110.00/$290.00.**
- ◆ **German Talking Barbie, $180.00/$350.00.**
- ◆ **Twist Barbie, $160.00/$340.00.**
- ◆ **Talking Christie, $130.00/ $230.00.**
- ◆ **Talking Stacey, $130.00/ $250.00.**
- ◆ **Twist Stacey, $140.00/$300.00.**
- ◆ **Two Twist Skipper dolls, $70.00/ $240.00 ea.**

1969

Truly Scrumptious, a Barbie size personality doll with a head from the Francie head mold, was offered in a Twist and a talking version. This doll, representing a character from the movie *Chitty Chitty Bang Bang*, was sold in only small numbers and is a desired and hard-to-find collectible today. In contrast the second personality doll of this year, Julia, after the character in the show of the same name, played by Diahann Carroll, was very popular in its time and can still be found easily. Julia comes either as a talking doll or in a Twist version (this year in a two piece nursing uniform). Some of these dolls have red oxidized hair, some heads keep their original brown color.

A few Julia dolls (and Christie dolls from 1970) were found with bright yellow hair. It is unknown whether these are prototypes, a result of oxidation, or treatment with chemicals (Color Magic solution?).

Another new friend of Barbie entered the scene, PJ, available this year only in a talking version.

The Barbie family went to the hairdresser. Twist Barbie as well as her friend Stacey and cousin Francie changed their hairdos to a shorter, curlier new look. Twist Skipper gets sausage curls and Standard Barbie a new one piece bathing suit.

After one year absence Ken joins the group again with a totally new look (Talking Ken and Spanish Talking Ken).

◆ **Julia with unusual yellow hair, $220.00, wearing Pink Fantasy, #1754, 1969, outfit, $45.00.**
◆ **Background Teen Dream Bedroom, 1971.**

♦ **Talking Truly Scrumptious (top faded), $250.00/$580.00.**
♦ **Straight Leg Truly Scrumptious, $220.00/$520.00.**
♦ **Talking PJ, two variations, each $90.00/$180.00.**

♦ **Talking Ken, $60.00/$120.00.**
♦ **Spanish Talking Ken, $70.00/$200.00.**

♦ **Twist Julia, $80.00/$200.00.**
♦ **Talking Julia, $80.00/$160.00.**

♦ Talking Julia in unusual shipping box (may be a promotional item), $80.00/$200.00.

♦ Standard Barbie, $150.00/$350.00.
♦ Twist Francie (notice unusual light haircolor), $160.00/$430.00; other haircolors, $130.00/$400.00.

♦ Twist Barbie, $150.00/$300.00.
♦ Twist Stacey, $130.00/$300.00.
♦ Twist Skipper, $100.00/$250.00.

1970

Barbie and her sister are more poseable than ever. Living Barbie and Skipper have a swivel waist and neck as well as poseable arms, elbows, hands, legs, knees, and low heel feet — most of which didn't last very long in the hands of children. These dolls are not very popular with collectors, with one exception: Living Barbie dolls that are produced in Japan, not in Taiwan as was the regular edition. There are two different types of these special Living Barbie dolls. One with light skin coloring and beautiful hair was produced exclusively for the Japanese market. The second one was sold in the U. S. in a gift set from Sears called "Action Accents" and has a more reddish lip color than the Taiwanese-made Living Barbie dolls. Also very hard to find is a Living Skipper made in Japan (not in Taiwan as nearly all Living Skipper dolls). She was offered only from Sears in the gift set "Very Best Velvet" (page 274). She has very coarse hair, a little bigger head, and different coloring than the regular line.

Five new characters were introduced 1970:
- Bendable Leg and Talking Brad, the first black male and a boyfriend for Christie (who changed her original dress to match Brad doll's outfit).
- Sears exclusive Jamie, she walks when a plate in her back is pushed. This doll was not a Department Special doll in Europe and is still easier to find over there, than in the U. S.
- Three companions for Tutti, called Pretty Pairs that each come with a toy of their own: Lori 'N Rori, Nan 'N Fran, and Angie 'N Tangie.

Talking Barbie gets a new, shorter hairdo. One very hard to find version of this doll has a head made from the Stacey head mold. PJ is now also offered as a Twist doll.

Ken with Bendable Legs, Twist Barbie, Stacey, Francie, Skipper, and new Twist Christie get redesigned bathing suits, Julia is sold in a new one-piece nursing uniform (which today is easier to find than the two-piece version). Two types of Francie dolls are introduced that have a hair theme: Hair Happenin's Francie and Francie with Growin' Pretty hair (issued with divided fingers).

- **Twist Stacey in Silver Serenade, #3419, 1971, $140.00.**

The re-issued first Skipper is also hard to find. She has a pinkish skin tone and differs from the Pink Skin Skipper from 1967 because of a larger, softer face and more vivid coloring. Her new box shows Mod outfits. The Japanese version of this doll again has unusual black and white eyes.

- Living Skipper, $40.00/$95.00.
- Japanese Living Barbie, $230.00/$500.00.
- Living Barbie, $90.00/$180.00.
- Talking Brad, $60.00/$110.00.
- Talking Christie, $75.00/$200.00.
- Living Barbie from Action Accents gift set, $280.00/$700.00.

- Hair Happenin's Francie, $110.00/$250.00.
- Walking Jamie, $120.00/$380.00.
- Francie with Growin' Pretty Hair, $70.00/$180.00.

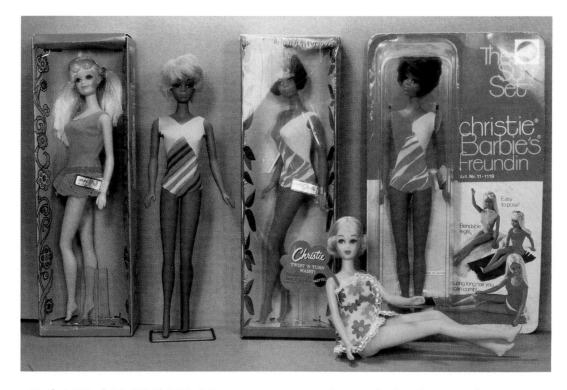

- Twist PJ, $80.00/$230.00.
- Twist Christie with yellow hair and unusual bathing suit, $250.00/$500.00. (Possibly foreign.)
- Twist Christie, $80.00/$180.00.
- Twist Francie, $130.00/$280.00.
- Twist Christie from Germany, $80.00/$300.00.

- Talking Stacey, $150.00/$380.00.
- Two Talking Barbie dolls, each $90.00/$230.00.
- Talking Barbie with Stacey head mold, $300.00/$450.00.
- Talking Ken, $50.00/$110.00.

- ◆ **New Good-Lookin' Ken, $40.00/$100.00.**
- ◆ **Brad, $45.00/$110.00.**
- ◆ **Julia, $70.00/$160.00.**
- ◆ **Twist Stacey, $170.00/$380.00.**
- ◆ **Twist Barbie, $140.00/$320.00.**

- ◆ **Japanese Skipper, $360.00/$520.00, wearing instead of the regular Skipper outfit the swim suit of a prototype black Skipper, swim suit only, $400.00.**
- ◆ **Lori 'N Rori, $120.00/$275.00.**
- ◆ **Angie 'N Tangie, $110.00/$230.00.**
- ◆ **Nan 'N Fran, $100.00/$210.00.**
- ◆ **Twist Skipper, $80.00/$210.00.**

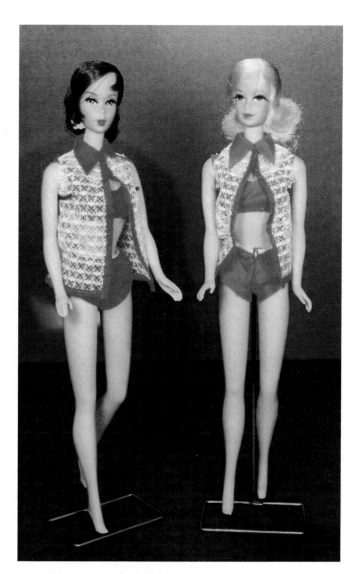

◆ **Closeup of this year's Talking Barbie dolls, notice the different colored swim suits.**

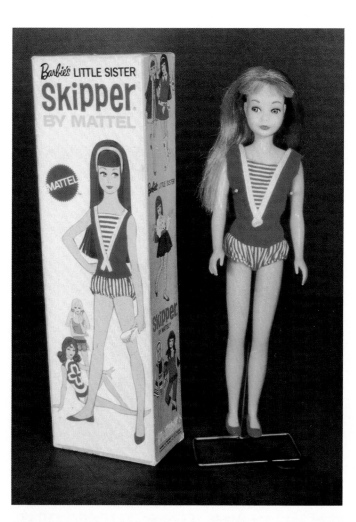

◆ **Re-issued Straight Leg Skipper, $70.00/ $200.00.**

1971

Groovy! Live Action Barbie, Ken, PJ, and (hardest to find) Christie look right out of Woodstock. They are accompanied either by a battery operated stage or a Touch N' Go stand.

The "hair game" is still very popular. Last year's Francie with Growin' Pretty hair gets new slender, undivided fingers. A matching Barbie is successful, Barbie with Growin' Pretty Hair.

A rarity today is Barbie Hair Happenin's with short red hair. She has new centered eyes in common with the new editions of these Barbie dolls: Standard, Twist N' Turn, Talking, and the Hair Fair head. Like most of these dolls Living Skipper gets new clothes — also a new friend, Living Fluff. Due to the type of vinyl used some heads of this year's Standard and Twist Barbie dolls fade, the ivory coloring often looks quite appealing.

Very popular, hard to find, and expensive is a Twist Francie with a new hairdo, No Bangs Francie.

Talking Julia goes to the hairdresser, too. The result is a fluffier bubble hairdo that retains its brown color. If found without a body these heads are distinguishable from Christie heads by the rooting pattern used. Julia doll's hairline goes from her forehead directly behind her ears while Christie has sort of sideburns.

- **Hair Fair Barbie in #3438 Peasant Dress, 1971, outfit, $60.00.**
- **Barbie doll's horse Dancer, $80.00.**
- **Live Action PJ in Gaucho Gear (vest and extra skirt not shown), #3436, 1971, outfit, $75.00.**

The Malibu series this year including Barbie, Ken, Francie, and Skipper, was a huge success but marked the beginning of the end of the "Golden Time of Vintage Barbie Dolls." The low budget dolls lack the quality (lashes, elaborate hairdos) and flair of the early Barbie dolls that collectors love so much. Malibu dolls stayed in the program for several years. During that time their hand molds and bathing suits underwent several changes.

1971

A very unusual doll with her big round head is Living Elli from Japan. As hard to find as Elli is a surprising Barbie from Australia. Mattel used some left over parts to create a new doll: head from the Barbie Hair Happenin's, old straight leg body (not quite matching in color), and a dress that had been sold exclusively in Japan.

A possible prototype is a Living Francie. She has the same body type as Busy Francie, the hands of Living Barbie, and the head mold and hair style of the earlier Twist Francie.

- ◆ **Live Action Barbie,** **$60.00/$140.00.**
- ◆ **Live Action Barbie on** **Stage, $90.00/$180.00.**
- ◆ **Live Action PJ,** **$60.00/$150.00.**
- ◆ **Live Action PJ on Stage,** **$100.00/$200.00.**

- ◆ **Francie with Growin'** **Pretty Hair, $60.00/** **$170.00.**
- ◆ **Live Action Ken,** **$50.00/$150.00.**
- ◆ **Live Action Ken** **on Stage, $110.00/** **$220.00.**
- ◆ **Live Action Christie,** **$100.00/$200.00.**
- ◆ **Barbie with Growin'** **Pretty Hair, $110.00/** **$250.00.**

- ◆ **Standard Barbie, $200.00/$400.00.**
- ◆ **Talking Julia with afro hair, $80.00/$170.00.**
- ◆ **Barbie Hair Happenin's, $450.00/ $900.00.**
- ◆ **Talking Barbie, $150.00/$300.00.**
- ◆ **Australian Hair Happenin's Barbie (pictured with wrong blouse) $500.00/$1,500.00.**

- ◆ **Living Skipper, $90.00/$200.00.**
- ◆ **Living Barbie, $130.00/$280.00.**
- ◆ **Living Fluff, $60.00/$150.00.**
- ◆ **Living Ellie from Japan, $500.00/ $1,200.00.**
- ◆ **Living Francie (prototype?), $400.00/$1,000.00.**

- ◆ **Two No Bangs Twist Francie dolls, each $600.00/$1,000.00.**
- ◆ **Two Twist Barbie dolls (note the unusual bathing suit of the blonde doll), $170.00/$390.00 each (add up to $70.00 for unusual bathing suits).**
- ◆ **Hair Fair set, $60.00/$110.00.**

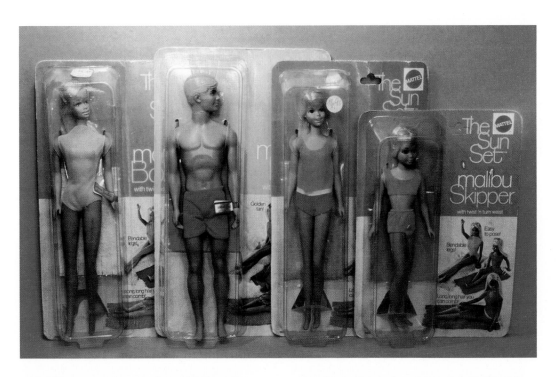

- ◆ **Malibu Barbie, $30.00/$60.00.**
- ◆ **Malibu Ken, $35.00/$65.00.**
- ◆ **Malibu Francie, $35.00/$65.00.**
- ◆ **Malibu Skipper, $25.00/$60.00.**

1972

This year marked the end of the highly collectible Twist era dolls. Three new series are introduced:

◆ Walk Lively (Barbie, Ken, Steffie, and Miss America) dolls with a special mechanism that turns the arms and head when the legs are moved by a Walk N' Turn stand.
◆ Busy (Barbie, Ken, Steffie, Francie) with hands that can open and close and are able to hold objects this way.
◆ Busy Talking (Barbie, Ken, Steffie) with the same busy hands and also a talking mechanism.

PJ, with a head made from the Midge head mold, joins the Malibu series.

Barbie with Growin' Pretty hair gets a less glamorous, more flower power looking dress and a slightly different hairdo.

Also available were: Pose N' Play Skipper (page 279) and her now hard-to-find friend Pose N' Play Tiff.

The most interesting U.S. Barbie of this year is Montgomery Ward's Anniversary Barbie. This doll was released to celebrate the department store's one hundredth birthday. She should resemble a No. 1 Barbie but looks more like a No. 5 Barbie.

A rarity is New Beautiful Francie. She was available (in a straight leg and a Busy version) only in Europe. Her unusual big round face has a strong resemblance to Japanese dolls (Elli).

◆ **In the middle: German Francie with straight legs, $500.00/$1,200.00, in First Formal, #1260, 1966, $100.00; and Busy German Francie, $600.00/$1,800.00, wearing Sweet 'N Swingin', #1283, $160.00.**
◆ **Accompanied by: brunette Twist Francie in Prom Pinks, #1295, 1967, dress, $170.00; Hair Happenin's Francie modeling Two for the Ball (purse is an addition), #1232, 1969, dress, $120.00.**
◆ **On the very right: Francie with Pretty Growin' Hair in Miss Teenage Beauty, #1284, 1967, dress, $350.00.**
◆ **Background Little Theatre.**

1972

- **Walk Lively Barbie, $70.00/$250.00.**
- **Walk Lively Steffie, $80.00/$260.00.**
- **Walk Lively Miss America $70.00/$160.00.**
- **Walk Lively Ken, $70.00/$160.00.**

- **Busy Steffie, $80.00/$250.00.**
- **Busy Ken from Europe with orange top, $110.00/$250.00.**
- **Busy Francie, $160.00/$250.00.**
- **Busy Ken (with red top), $60.00/$140.00.**

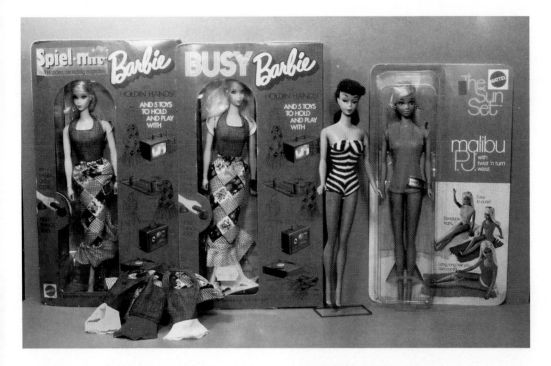

- ◆ **Spiel mit Barbie (German Busy Barbie), $60.00/$350.00.**
- ◆ **Busy Barbie, $60.00/$250.00 (note the three different body suits).**
- ◆ **Montgomery Ward's Barbie, $500.00/$700.00.**
- ◆ **Malibu PJ, $30.00/$60.00.**

- ◆ **Barbie with Growin' Pretty Hair, $120.00/$270.00.**
- ◆ **Talking Busy Steffie, $120.00/$350.00.**
- ◆ **Talking Busy Barbie, with longer or shorter hair, each $80.00/$260.00.**
- ◆ **Talking Busy Ken, $70.00/$200.00.**
- ◆ **Pose 'N Play Tiff, $150.00/$300.00.**

1973

Most of the dolls from this and the following years have not been discovered by mainstream collectors and can still be found for relatively low prices.

Quick Curl dolls are the big hit in 1973. Thin wires in the hair material make the styling easy. Quick Curl Barbie, her red haired friend Kelley, Francie, Skipper, and brunette Miss America are joined by Mod Hair Ken. He is the first adult male doll with rooted hair and comes with reusable beard pieces. He is available with two different types of heads, a small hard one or a larger and softer head.

A new edition to the Malibu line is Malibu Christie.

Some leftover dolls and mute talkers from earlier years were repackaged into plastic bags and sold very cheaply as "Baggies."

- ◆ **Baggie Ken, $50.00/$90.00.**
- ◆ **Baggie PJ, $60.00/$100.00.**
- ◆ **Baggie Skipper, $45.00/$70.00.**

- Quick Curl Barbie, $35.00/$70.00.
- Quick Curl Skipper, $30.00/$65.00.
- Quick Curl Francie, $65.00/$100.00.
- Quick Curl Kelley, $45.00/$100.00.

- Two versions of Mod Hair Ken, each $25.00/$50.00. Notice the three variations of the original jacket.
- Prototype head of Mod Hair Ken, $200.00.
- Malibu Christie, $25.00/$60.00.
- Quick Curl Miss America, $75.00/$150.00.

1974

With the Olympics just two years away and sports more popular than ever Mattel creates a sport series, the Sports Set. Yellowstone Kelley is the only special doll in this line. Sun Valley Barbie and Ken as well as Newport Barbie are just regular Malibu dolls in sporting outfits.

A big event (with enormous publicity coverage) is Barbie doll's 16th birthday. To celebrate, a special doll is created: Sweet 16 Barbie.

Quick Curl Miss America is now also available in blonde.

Montgomery Ward offers a dressed Mod Hair Ken (Montgomery Ward Ken). Another Department Store special is the new Barbie Baby Sits set from Sears. The baby is the same one as used for The Sunshine Family (another Mattel product but not Barbie related).

- ◆ **Yellowstone Kelley, $140.00/$325.00.**
- ◆ **Sun Valley Barbie, $40.00/$110.00.**
- ◆ **Sun Valley Ken, $30.00/$90.00.**

- ◆ **Sweet 16 Barbie promo from Germany, $35.00/$100.00.**
- ◆ **Two Newport Barbie dolls, $40.00/$100.00 each.**
- ◆ **Sweet 16 Barbie, $35.00/ $75.00.**
- ◆ **Quick Curl Miss America, $55.00/$95.00.**

Funtime dolls, Barbie, Ken, Skipper, and hardest to find Skooter are only available in Europe and Canada. In these countries four other budget dolls are also offered:

◆ No. 8587 Barbie, with blonde hair, yellow bathing suit in Canada, blue bathing suit and old Barbie hand mold in Europe.

◆ No. 8587 Barbie (same stock number as blonde doll) with red hair and Stacey head mold with teeth, hard to find.

◆ No. 8588 Barbie, a very unusual doll with the old TNT Barbie head mold, bendable legs, and a straight waist.

◆ No. 8126 Skipper, just a Funtime Skipper in a different colored bathing suit.

◆ **Montgomery Ward's Ken, $65.00/$130.00.**
◆ **Baby Sits set, $25.00/$45.00.**
◆ **Funtime Ken, $25.00/$60.00.**
◆ **Funtime Barbie, $30.00/$70.00.**
◆ **Funtime Skipper, $25.00/$55.00.**
◆ **Funtime Skooter, $130.00/$200.00. (All Funtime available only in Europe and Canada.)**

◆ **Three Barbie dolls with the same stock number, 8587. Blonde, $20.00/ 50.00; red-haired, $100.00/ $200.00.**
◆ **No. 8126 Skipper, $40.00/$80.00.**
◆ **No. 8588 Barbie, $100.00/$200.00. (All available only in Europe and Canada.)**

1975

When the Olympic popularity reaches its peak Mattel introduces the Gold Medal line of dolls: Gold Medal Barbie and Ken, Barbie Skier, Barbie Skater, PJ Gymnast, and Ken Skier. Foreign dolls often represent their countries in different colored bathing suits. Skipper could be found only in Europe.

Free Moving dolls have a special tab in their back that when pulled out gives them an easier posability. Barbie, Ken, and PJ now have two new black friends, Free Moving Cara and Brad. Cara is also available in a Quick Curl Version.

Two more Baggie dolls are offered. Contrary to the earlier ones, they are created especially to be Baggie dolls. Casey is dressed either in a pink or a rare red bikini.

The first Hawaiian Barbie is made from the Steffie head mold and had Francie type arms.

The most unusual and controversial U.S. doll of this year is Growing Up Skipper. By turning her arm around she grows about ¾ of an inch, developing a bustline.

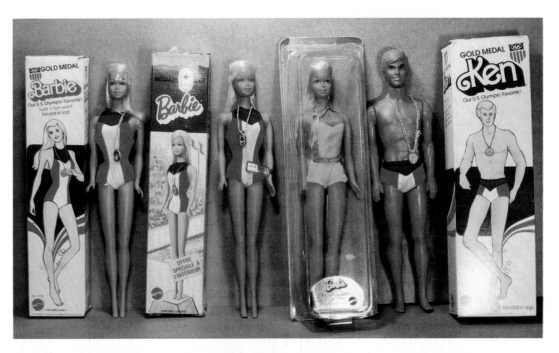

Most interesting are the dolls from abroad.

In Japan two new round headed dolls are offered: Butterfly Skipper and Tulip Francie, made by Kohusai Mattel Ltd. Japan.

In Germany Tutti, Chris, and Todd are still available, but they now come in very hard-to-find outfits (for only one year). At the same time three re-issued Tutti playsets are offered in this country: Swing a Ling, Night-Night Sleep Tight, and Me and My Doll. The accessories are mostly the same as in the old playsets, but the colors changed. The dolls coming with these sets, as well as any later dolls in this size, differ greatly from their predecessors. Their heads are much smaller and harder. The bodies, that are not easy to bend, are either not marked at all or marked only Hong Kong. In England a new re-issued Todd is already available this year. He also comes in a very hard-to-find outfit.

- **Gold Medal Barbie, $40.00/$90.00.**
- **Gold Medal Barbie from Canada (notice the different medal), $45.00/$85.00.**
- **Gold Medal Barbie from Australia, $50.00/$90.00.**
- **Gold Medal Ken, $25.00/$60.00.**

- ◆ **Gold Medal Gymnast PJ, $40.00/$90.00.**
- ◆ **Gold Medal Skipper (Europe), $55.00/$90.00.**
- ◆ **Gold Medal Skipper (Italy), $60.00/$95.00.**

- ◆ **Gold Medal Barbie Skier, $45.00/$95.00.**
- ◆ **Gold Medal Barbie Skater, $45.00/$95.00.**
- ◆ **Gold Medal Ken Skier, $30.00/$70.00.**

◆ **Free Moving Barbie, $35.00/$75.00.**
◆ **Free Moving Cara, $40.00/$75.00.**
◆ **Free Moving Curtis, $50.00/$85.00.**

◆ **Quick Curl Cara, $50.00/$90.00.**
◆ **Free Moving Ken, $35.00/$70.00.**
◆ **Free Moving PJ, $40.00/$75.00.**

- ◆ **Baggie Casey in rare red swim suit, $80.00/$150.00.**
- ◆ **Baggie Casey in pink swim suit, $45.00/$80.00.**
- ◆ **Baggie Francie, $55.00/$110.00.**

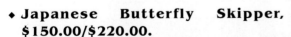

- ◆ **Japanese Butterfly Skipper, $150.00/$220.00.**
- ◆ **Japanese Tulip Francie, $150.00/ $250.00.**

- ◆ **Hawaiian Barbie, $35.00/$70.00.**
- ◆ **Night-Night Sleep Tight set (Germany), $100.00/$200.00.**
- ◆ **Swing A Ling set (Germany), $120.00/$220.00.**
- ◆ **Growing Up Skipper, $30.00/$65.00.**
- ◆ **Me and My Dolly set (Germany), $150.00/$250.00.**

- ◆ **Todd from England, $65.00/$120.00.**
- ◆ **German Chris, $130.00/$250.00.**
- ◆ **German Todd, $85.00/$150.00.**
- ◆ **German Tutti, $90.00/$170.00.**

1976

This year starts with a new logo for Barbie.

1973's Quick Curl dolls got a make-over and are now offered as Deluxe Quick Curl Barbie, Cara, Skipper (only available in Europe), and new PJ.

1973's Mod Hair Ken is replaced by Now Look Ken, available in two hair lengths and different hand molds.

Nice additions to every collection are Ballerina Barbie and Cara. A special mechanism inside their bodies allows them to lift up one leg when the body is bent a little backwards. Ballerina Barbie is offered also in a Ballerina Barbie On Tour set with an extra outfit.

Skipper gets a new friend, Growing Up Ginger.

This year's rarest doll is Beautiful Bride Barbie with real lashes.

A budget doll with the Stacy head mold is available in Germany in a blue bikini (#7382), and in the U.S. in an orange bathing suit (Barbie Plus 3).

Re-issued Tutti, Todd, and Chris replace last year's models in Europe. Todd from now on is available with brown or red hair, Tutti in blonde, and Chris in brunette or with red hair. The cutest little edition is Carla. Although most of these hard-to-find dolls have bangs, a few without bangs have been found.

◆ **Ballerina Barbie On Tour, $45.00/$85.00.**

- ◆ **Deluxe Quick Curl Barbie, $35.00/$65.00.**
- ◆ **Deluxe Quick Curl Cara, $35.00/$65.00.**
- ◆ **Deluxe Quick Curl PJ, $45.00/$90.00.**
- ◆ **Deluxe Quick Curl Skipper (Europe), $65.00/$110.00.**

- ◆ **Two Now Look Ken dolls, each $35.00/$65.00.**
- ◆ **Ballerina Barbie, $25.00/$50.00.**
- ◆ **Ballerina Cara, $40.00/$75.00.**

- **Beautiful Bride Barbie, $140.00/ $250.00.**
- **No. 7382 (or Barbie Plus 3) $10.00/ $25.00.**
- **Growing Up Ginger, $45.00/$80.00.**

- **Tutti, dress with yellow bow (Europe), $45.00/$75.00.**
- **Chris, red haired (Europe), $50.00/ $85.00.**
- **Late 1976, early 1977 Chris (has new box but older type dress) (Europe), $50.00/$90.00.**

- **Tutti, dress with blue bow (Europe), $40.00/$70.00.**
- **Chris, brunette (Europe), $45.00/$80.00.**
- **Todd (Europe), $55.00/$95.00.**
- **Carla without bangs (Europe), $100.00/$150.00.**
- **Carla (Europe), $75.00/ $120.00.**

1977

Barbie doll's third major facelift results in the popular SuperStar face, that is still used today. It is named after this year's SuperStar Barbie. The same mold is used also for SuperStar Christie and on a bigger scale for SuperSize Barbie, SuperSize Christie, and SuperSize Barbie Bride.

Donny and Marie Osmond, popular TV celebrities, are the models for two new personality dolls.

This year's cheapest doll is Sweet 16. It is questionable whether she should be considered part of the Barbie family or not, because she is not named Barbie. This doll is made by Mattel, has a Barbie body, Barbie bathing suit, and a Barbie family head (head mold like Japanese Elli or German Francie). The outfits available for her are either Barbie outfits or variations of these.

Three new versions of Hawaiian Barbie are offered in department stores.

- ◆ **SuperStar Barbie, $45.00/$80.00.**
- ◆ **SuperStar Barbie, German promo doll, $50.00/$95.00.**
- ◆ **SuperStar Barbie from Japan, $50.00/$100.00.**
- ◆ **SuperStar Barbie, $50.00/$95.00.**

- ◆ **Donny and Marie Osmond set, $40.00/$85.00 (dolls separate, each $20.00/$35.00).**
- ◆ **Donny and Marie Osmond outfits, each $15.00/$25.00.**

Again many interesting dolls are not available in the U.S.: Equestrienne Barbie has the body of a Living Barbie, hands of a Busy Barbie, and the old Twist era face mold. She is offered in Canada and Europe.

Another interesting Barbie, available in Germany, Italy, France, and this year in Canada, is Partytime Barbie, known in several versions and two different outfits. They all have real lashes. This year's model has the Twist head mold and wears a metallic and orange outfit.

In Europe only a re-issued Hair Fair head with painted lashes and a cheap Barbie (again #7382) is sold.

The re-issued European Tutti, Todd, and Chris get new outfits. Of these dolls, only Tutti is sold in Canada.

◆ **Sweet 16, $10.00/$35.00.**
◆ **Sweet 16 outfits, each $8.00/$20.00.**

◆ **Three versions of Hawaiian Barbie, each $20.00/$55.00.**

1977

◆ **SuperSize Barbie, $150.00/$250.00.**
◆ **SuperSize Barbie Bride, $200.00/$350.00.**
◆ **SuperSize Christie, $180.00/$280.00.**

◆ **SuperStar Christie, $45.00/$80.00.**
◆ **Equestrienne Barbie (Europe), $75.00/$125.00.**
◆ **Equestrienne Barbie (Italy), note the wrist tag, $70.00/$130.00.**
◆ **No. 7382 Barbie (Europe), $25.00 – 45.00.**

◆ **Three Partytime Barbie dolls (Europe and Canada), each $50.00/$75.00.**
◆ **Hair Fair set (Europe), $50.00/$120.00.**

◆ **Todd (Europe), $55.00/$95.00.**
◆ **Tutti (Europe), $36.00/$65.00.**
◆ **Chris (Europe), $45.00/$80.00.**

1978

Fashion Photo Barbie, Christie, and PJ can be remote-controlled. A play-camera is connected by wire to the doll stand. Inside the doll an inner mechanism allows lifelike movements resembling those of a high fashion model.

Last year's SuperStar Barbie, now available in a gift package with extra outfits, is joined by SuperStar Ken. A Malibu Barbie with extra outfits has the name Malibu Barbie Fashion Combo.

Four new personality dolls enter the scene: Jimmy Osmond, Kitty O'Neil, and Cheryl Ladd and Kate Jackson from the TV hit *Charlie's Angels.*

In Europe the Spiel mit (Play With) line with Ken, Skipper, and Barbie with a Stacey head mold, are introduced.

The all-time favorite foreign doll seems to be SuperStar Hawaiian Barbie. Contrary to the regular Hawaiian Barbie dolls she has luscious long hair, a nice outfit and accessories, a lei made out of fabric, and quality workmanship. In the same line, Picture Pretty Barbie, a regular SuperStar Barbie in a new outfit, is accompanied by a TV camera and lights. The last doll in this line is Beautiful Bride Barbie (available also in a few U.S. department stores). In contrast to the 1976 U.S. Beautiful Bride Barbie, she has the

- ◆ **Hawaiian SuperStar Barbie (Europe), $140.00/$250.00.**
- ◆ **Picture Pretty Barbie (Europe), $70.00/$110.00.**
- ◆ **Beautiful Bride Barbie, $65.00/$90.00.**

new face mold and painted, not rooted lashes. These Barbie dolls are the first European dolls that are packaged in special multilingual boxes (available also in Canada).

This year's Partytime Barbie (in a new outfit) is joined by Partytime Skipper (with real lashes, too), and Partytime Ken. For these Ken dolls the Talking Ken body mold is used, but the holes in the back have not been cut out (they can be seen). Partytime Skipper and Barbie are offered only in Europe, Ken is also offered in Canada.

In Spain SuperStar Barbie is sold in a different outfit and box.

♦ **Fashion Photo Barbie, $30.00/$60.00.**
♦ **Fashion Photo PJ, $50.00/$80.00.**

♦ **Fashion Photo Christie, $35.00/$65.00.**
♦ **Spiel mit Ken (Europe), $25.00/$45.00.**
♦ **Spiel mit Skipper (Europe), $35.00/$55.00.**
♦ **Spiel mit Barbie (Europe), $40.00/$65.00.**

1978

- ◆ **SuperStar Ken, $35.00/$55.00.**
- ◆ **Jimmy Osmond, $35.00/$55.00.**
- ◆ **Malibu Barbie Fashion Combo, $30.00/$55.00.**

- ◆ **SuperStar Barbie Fashion Change-abouts, $50.00/$85.00.**
- ◆ **SuperStar Barbie from Spain, $65.00/$100.00.**

- ◆ **Three Partytime Barbie dolls (Europe), $50.00/$75.00.**
- ◆ **Two Partytime Ken dolls (Europe and Canada), $45.00/$70.00.**
- ◆ **Partytime Skipper (Europe), $70.00/$100.00.**

- ◆ **Kate Jackson, $35.00/$65.00.**
- ◆ **Kitty O'Neil, $35.00/$65.00.**
- ◆ **Cheryl Ladd, $35.00/$65.00.**

1979

Kissing Barbie and Christie are this year's most unusual dolls. By pressing a plate in the neck the doll's head tilts and her lips pucker. When released the sound of a kiss can be heard. Pretty Changes Barbie is a nice doll with unusual short hair and interchangeable wigs.

The all new Super Teen Skipper comes with a helmet and a skateboard.

Only available for a short period of time and now hard to find is SuperSize Barbie with Super Hair. This doll has Quick Curl Hair and a section of her hair could be lengthened and shortened.

◆ **SuperSize Barbie with Super Hair, $170.00/$270.00.**

Dolls from the Malibu line underwent countless changes through the years. This year's dolls, Sun Lovin', Ken, PJ, Christie, and Skipper have a painted on suntan, the skin under their bathing suits is lighter, than the skin exposed to the sun.

To the delight of many collectors, two new personality dolls are released: Debby Boone and Kristy McNichol (from the TV show *Family*).

Matching the still available Hawaiian Barbie is Hawaiian Ken.

Very interesting and surprising are MoonMystic and SunSpell. Considered to be part of the Barbie line, these Guardian Goddesses were only available in a few test market areas in the U.S. and are highly collectible today.

Strandspass (Beachfun) Barbie, Ken, and Skipper are found in Europe and in Canada at Sears.

Available in Europe only is Equestrienne Barbie with the SuperStar head mold. Even though Equestrienne Barbie dolls with this head mold are harder to find than the earlier ones with the Twist Barbie mold, these dolls are not as popular for collectors as the first version.

Another re-issue of the Hair Fair head, only available in Europe and Canada, has the SuperStar head mold and comes in a new, pink box. This year's No. 7382 Barbie has a new face mold, too.

A mystery Skipper doll, found in a flea market in Paris, has lashes and comes in an outfit that resembles Starr dresses (Starr is another Mattel doll, not considered to belong to the Barbie family).

- ◆ **Kissing Barbie, $20.00/$50.00.**
- ◆ **Kissing Christie, $30.00/$60.00.**
- ◆ **Pretty Changes Barbie, $25.00/$50.00.**
- ◆ **7382 Barbie (Europe), $15.00/$35.00.**

- ◆ **Debby Boone, $35.00/$65.00.**
- ◆ **Kristy McNichol, $40.00/$70.00.**

1979

- ◆ **Sun Lovin' Ken, $8.00/$15.00.**
- ◆ **Sun Lovin' PJ, $10.00/$20.00.**
- ◆ **Sun Lovin' Barbie, $8.00/$15.00.**
- ◆ **Sun Lovin' Christie, $10.00/$20.00.**
- ◆ **Sun Lovin' Skipper, $8.00/$15.00.**

- ◆ **Hawaiian Ken, $25.00/$45.00.**
- ◆ **Super Teen Skipper, $15.00/$35.00.**
- ◆ **Unknown French Skipper, $70.00/$100.00.**
- ◆ **Hair Happening Set (Europe and Canada), $35.00/$70.00.**

◆ **MoonMystic, $90.00/$125.00.**
◆ **SunSpell, $95.00/$130.00.**

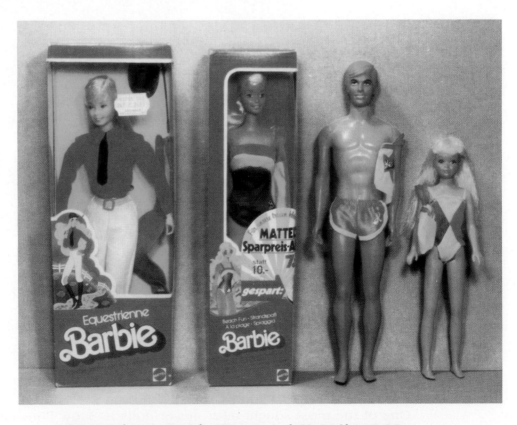

◆ **Equestrienne Barbie (Europe), $70.00/$115.00.**
◆ **Beach Fun Barbie (Europe and Canada), $15.00/$30.00.**
◆ **Beach Fun Ken (Europe and Canada), $15.00/$30.00.**
◆ **Beach Fun Skipper (Europe and Canada), $20.00/$35.00.**

1980

This year's leading dolls, Beauty Secrets Barbie and Christie can move their arms when a place in their back is pushed.

A new tradition is started in 1980 — the release of Dolls of the World Barbie dolls every year. First in the line are Italian Barbie, Parisian Barbie, and Royal Barbie. The last one was offered in Europe as Princess Barbie. Black Barbie is in reality the first colored Barbie ever. Before black dolls were different characters (Christie, Cara, Julia). From this year on Barbie started to have several ethnic backgrounds, as with Hispanic Barbie (called Rio Senjorita Barbie in Europe). Skipper (finally) gets a new boyfriend, Scott, who has rooted hair. Sport & Shave Ken is an unusual doll. He, too, has rooted hair and Big Jim (a Mattel doll for boys) type arms.

Following the newest trend Mattel introduces Roller Skating Barbie and Ken.

A regular Malibu Barbie comes with a special case and accessories in The Malibu Barbie Beach Party.

In Germany two new budget lines are introduced: Sports Star and Jeans. Both consisted of Barbie, Ken, and Skipper. In Canada only the Barbie dolls were sold.

- ◆ **Royal Barbie $120.00/$200.00.**
- ◆ **Dog sled (Europe), $80.00/$150.00.**
- ◆ **Snow Princess Barbie (Finland and Sweden), $150.00/$240.00.**

A Canadian special doll is Barbie No. 7382-0710, a Barbie Plus 3 as a dressed doll in different outfits.

A French personality doll portrays a famous French singer, Chantal Goya.

One of the most sought after newer dolls is Snow Princess Barbie, sold only in Finland and Sweden. The matching dog sled is also offered in Germany as part of the Big Jim line.

♦ **Beauty Secrets Barbie Pretty Reflections, $45.00/ $75.00.**
♦ **Beauty Secrets Barbie from Spain, $50.00/$80.00.**
♦ **Beauty Secrets Barbie, $35.00/$50.00.**

♦ **Malibu Barbie The Beach Party, $40.00/$65.00.**

♦ **Beauty Secrets Christie, $45.00/$65.00.**
♦ **Sport & Shave Ken, $35.00/$50.00.**
♦ **Scott, $30.00/$45.00.**

1980

- ◆ **Italian Barbie, $120.00/$200.00.**
- ◆ **Parisian Barbie, $90.00/$140.00.**
- ◆ **Princess Barbie (Europe), $95.00/$150.00.**

- ◆ **Black (Ebony) Christie, $35.00/$55.00.**
- ◆ **Rio Senjorita (Hispanic) Barbie, $35.00/$50.00.**
- ◆ **Senjorita Barbie from Spain, $45.00/$65.00.**
- ◆ **Chantal Goya (France), $70.00/$100.00.**

- ◆ Two No. 7382 Canadian Barbie dolls, each $20.00/$35.00.
- ◆ Roller Skating Barbie, $25.00/$45.00.
- ◆ Roller Skating Ken, $25.00/$45.00.

- ◆ Jeans Ken (Germany), $15.00/$30.00.
- ◆ Jeans Barbie (Germany), $15.00/$30.00.
- ◆ Jeans Skipper (Germany), $20.00/$35.00.
- ◆ Sports Star Ken (Germany), $15.00/$30.00.
- ◆ Sports Star Barbie (Germany), $15.00/$30.00.
- ◆ Sports Star Skipper (Germany), $20.00/$35.00.

1981

This year marks the introduction of two new dolls that stayed on the market (in different issues) for quite a few years: My First Barbie, this special Barbie for the small girl has extra smooth legs for easier dressing, and Birthday Barbie, with a little gift for the birthday girl. The new Dolls of the World Barbie dolls are Scottish and Oriental.

Golden Girl Barbie and Christie, this year's leading dolls, can be found with several different hairstyles, outfit variations, and arm molds. Also Western Barbie (with an inner mechanism that allows the doll to wink with one eyelid when a button in her back is pressed) has a variety of hairstyles. The European version of this doll can't wink. She is basically the same doll as the second edition Equestrienne Barbie but without bangs. She has a Living Barbie type body, busy hands, and a regular SuperStar face.

Germany again has several budget line dolls: Playtime Barbie, Disco Barbie, Ken, and Skipper. Disco Ken and Barbie are sold in Canada, too. In Denmark and Australia a Safari line is offered. English children could look forward to two promotional My First Barbie dolls.

- ◆ **Golden Dream Barbie Special, $50.00/$90.00.**
- ◆ **Two Golden Dream Barbie dolls, each $20.00/$40.00.**
- ◆ **Golden Dream Barbie with straight arms, $25.00/ $45.00.**

- ◆ **Three Western Barbie dolls with different hairstyles, each $20.00/$35.00.**
- ◆ **Western Barbie from Europe, $50.00/$70.00.**

- ◆ **Western Skipper, $20.00/$35.00.**
- ◆ **Western Ken, $15.00/$32.00.**
- ◆ **Playtime Barbie (Germany), $15.00/$25.00.**
- ◆ **Golden Dream Christie, $30.00/$45.00.**

- ◆ **My First Barbie promo from Germany, $12.00/$25.00.**
- ◆ **Two My First Barbie dolls from England, $20.00/$50.00.**

◆ **Feliz Cumpleaños Barbie from Spain, $40.00/$55.00.**
◆ **Happy Birthday Barbie, $10.00/$25.00.**
◆ **Scottish Barbie, $90.00/$140.00.**
◆ **Oriental Barbie, $80.00/$110.00.**

◆ **Disco Ken (Germany and Canada), $15.00/$30.00.**
◆ **Disco Barbie (Germany and Canada), $15.00/$30.00.**
◆ **Disco Skipper (Germany), $20.00/$35.00.**
◆ **Safari Barbie (Denmark and Australia), $25.00/$40.00.**
◆ **Safari Skipper (Denmark and Australia), $25.00/$40.00.**

1982

This year's most elegant dolls are Pink & Pretty Barbie and her friend Christie.

Magic Curl Barbie and Christie have an unusual hairdo. Their short curly hair can be straightened by a chemical solution.

Eskimo and India Barbie are the first dolls from the Dolls of the World line that are also sold in Canada.

All Star Ken with painted hair is the successor to 1980's Sport Star Ken. Also available are Fashion Jeans Barbie and Ken.

A new Malibu line, Sunsational Malibu is introduced, consisting of: Barbie, PJ, Hispanic Barbie, Christie (with two different head molds), Ken, black Ken (with painted or harder to find rooted hair), and Skipper.

Jogging Skipper is sold exclusively in Europe, Barbie and Ken from this line are also available in Canada.

An unusual gift set, offered only in France, is "Barbie et son chien Prince." The dog is either accompanied by a Hispanic (Rio Senjorita Barbie) or a Magic Curl Barbie.

- ◆ **Pink & Pretty Barbie from England, $25.00/$90.00.**
- ◆ **Pink & Pretty Barbie Special, $30.00/$80.00 (regular edition $25.00/$35.00.**
- ◆ **Pink & Pretty Christie, $35.00/$45.00.**

1982

- Magic Curl Barbie, $25.00/$35.00.
- Barbie Rizos from Spain, $40.00/$55.00.
- Magic Curl Barbie, black, $30.00/$45.00.

- India Barbie, $90.00/$135.00.
- Eskimo Barbie, $85.00/$125.00.
- All Star Ken, $25.00/$40.00.

- ◆ **Sunsational Malibu Barbie, $8.00/$18.00.**
- ◆ **Sunsational Malibu PJ, $10.00/$20.00.**
- ◆ **Sunsational Malibu Hispanic Barbie, $12.00/$25.00.**
- ◆ **Two Sunsational Malibu Christie dolls (different head mold), each $12.00/$25.00.**

- ◆ **Sunsational Malibu Ken, $8.00/$18.00.**
- ◆ **Sunsational Malibu black Ken with rooted hair, $35.00/$50.00.**
- ◆ **Sunsational Malibu black Ken with painted hair, $12.00/$25.00.**
- ◆ **Sunsational Malibu Skipper, $8.00/$18.00.**

1982

◆ **Barbie et son chien Prince set from France, $70.00/ $150.00.**

◆ **Jogging Barbie (Europe and Canada), $15.00/$30.00.**
◆ **Jogging Ken (Europe and Canada), $15.00/$30.00.**
◆ **Jogging Skipper (Europe), $20.00/$35.00.**
◆ **Fashion Jeans Barbie, $20.00/$35.00.**
◆ **Fashion Jeans Ken, $15.00/$30.00.**

In 1983 little girls could look forward to:

- Dream Date Barbie, PJ, and Ken.
- Western Barbie doll's successor Horse Lovin' Barbie. She doesn't wink. The European version has a Living Barbie type body and busy hands. Ken and Skipper are the same in the U.S. and Europe.
- Twirly Curl Barbie in white, black, and Hispanic.
- Tracy and Todd (Barbie doll's friends, bride and groom).
- Angle Face Barbie.
- Swedish and Spanish Barbie dolls in the Dolls of the World line.
- Hawaiian Barbie and Ken in new issues.
- Barbie and Friends gift set with PJ, Ken, and Barbie in one box.
- Ballerina Barbie re-issued with a SuperStar face.
- Barbie and Ken Campin' Out Set.
- A rare Bridal Barbie sold only in Europe (a SuperStar-type Barbie wearing Tracy's bridal gown).
- A foreign Super Dance Barbie and Ken offered in Canada. European children can play with these and a matching Skipper.
- Partytime Barbie (a My First Barbie in one-piece suit) sold in Canada and Europe.
- No. 5336 Barbie. This beautiful doll from Germany has lovely reddish hair and straight legs and has been found in three different outfit variations.
- City Barbie, also sold in Germany.
- A Wayne Gretzky personality doll available only in Canada.

- **Dream Date Barbie, $20.00/$35.00.**
- **Barbie Gran Gala from Spain, $45.00/$65.00.**
- **Dream Date PJ, $30.00/$45.00.**

- ◆ Horse Lovin' Ken, $20.00/$40.00.
- ◆ Horse Lovin' Skipper, $20.00/$40.00.
- ◆ Dream Date Ken, $15.00/$30.00.

- ◆ Horse Lovin' Barbie, $20.00/$40.00.
- ◆ Horse Lovin' Barbie from Europe, $50.00/$70.00.
- ◆ Horse Lovin' Barbie from Spain, $45.00/$60.00.

◆ **Twirly Curls Barbie, $20.00/$40.00.**
◆ **Twirly Curls Barbie Gift Set, $45.00/ $80.00.**

◆ **Twirly Curls Barbie, black, $25.00/$45.00.**
◆ **Twirly Curls Barbie, Hispanic, $25.00/$45.00.**

◆ **Barbie and Friends set, $40.00/$60.00.**
◆ **Ballerina Barbie, $40.00/$60.00.**

1983

- Tracy, $30.00/$45.00.
- Todd, $30.00/$45.00.
- Bridal Barbie (Europe), $50.00/$80.00.

- Angel Face Barbie, $16.00/$25.00.
- Swedish Barbie, $60.00/$90.00.
- Spanish Barbie, $65.00/$100.00.

◆ **Hawaiian Barbie, $15.00/$25.00.**
◆ **Hawaiian Ken, $15.00/$25.00.**
◆ **Wayne Gretzky from Canada, $80.00/$140.00.**

◆ **Barbie and Friends Campin' Out Set, $40.00/$60.00.**
◆ **Partytime Barbie (Europe and Canada), $15.00/$25.00.**

- **Two Super Dance Barbie dolls (Europe), $15.00/$25.00.**
- **Super Dance Barbie from Spain, $20.00/$35.00.**
- **Super Dance Skipper (Europe), $20.00/$35.00.**
- **Super Dance Ken (Europe and Canada), $15.00/$25.00.**

- **Three No. 5336 Barbie dolls (Germany), each $20.00/$30.00.**
- **City Barbie (Germany), $20.00/$30.00.**

1984

New dolls available are:
- Crystal Barbie and Ken (each in black and white) and in Italy only Crystal Christie.
- Sweet Roses PJ.
- Happy Birthday Barbie in a new issue.
- Loving You Barbie.
- Great Shape Barbie, black Barbie, Ken, and Skipper. In England and Canada these dolls are available in green outfits, in England even in a gift set. Some Great Shape Barbie dolls and Skipper dolls sold in France and Spain for the local markets are produced in these countries and have a softer look.
- Irish and Swiss Barbie from the Dolls of the World series.
- A new Malibu line — Sun Gold Malibu Barbie, PJ, Hispanic Barbie, black Barbie, Ken, Hispanic Ken, black Ken, and Skipper.

From Europe and Canada:
- Fabulous Fur (Festival) Barbie and the first line of Fashion Play Barbie dolls. The ones produced in France again have a different face coloring.
- Ken Ceremonie available in France only.
- Pretty Party Barbie from England, which is another My First Barbie in a new dress.

- **Crystal Barbie, $15.00/$25.00.**
- **Crystal Barbie, black, $20.00/$30.00.**
- **Mille Luci Christie (Italy), $20.00/$55.00.**

- ◆ Crystal Ken, $15.00/$25.00.
- ◆ Crystal Ken, black, $20.00/$30.00.
- ◆ Sweet Roses PJ, $25.00/$40.00.
- ◆ Happy Birthday Barbie, $15.00/$25.00.

- ◆ Loving You Barbie Special, $25.00/$50.00.
- ◆ Loving You Barbie, $20.00/$30.00.
- ◆ Barbie Corazon from Spain, $40.00/$50.00.

- ◆ Irish Barbie, $60.00/$95.00.
- ◆ Swiss Barbie, $55.00/$80.00.
- ◆ Fabulous Fur (Festival) Barbie (Europe and Canada), $30.00/$50.00.

- ◆ Great Shape Barbie, $10.00/$20.00.
- ◆ Star Super Danse 2 Barbie from France, $20.00/$40.00.
- ◆ Ritmic Barbie from Spain, $20.00/$40.00.
- ◆ Aeróbica Barbie from Mexico, $20.00/$40.00.

- **Great Shape Barbie, black, $12.00/$23.00.**
- **Ritmic Skipper from Spain, $20.00/$40.00.**
- **Great Shape Skipper, $8.00/$18.00.**

- **Great Shape gift set from England, $45.00/$100.00.**
- **Great Shape Ken, $8.00/$18.00.**

◆ **Two Sun Gold Malibu Barbie dolls, each $5.00/$15.00.**
◆ **Sun Gold Malibu PJ, $8.00/$18.00.**
◆ **Sun Gold Malibu Hispanic Barbie, $8.00/$18.00.**
◆ **Sun Gold Malibu black Barbie, $8.00/$18.00.**

◆ **Sun Gold Malibu Ken, $5.00/$10.00.**
◆ **Sun Gold Malibu Hispanic Ken, $8.00/$18.00.**
◆ **Sun Gold Malibu black Ken, $8.00/$18.00.**
◆ **Sun Gold Malibu Skipper, $5.00/$10.00.**

◆ **Five Fashion Play Barbie dolls (Europe and Canada), each $10.00/$20.00.**

◆ **Pretty Party Barbie from England, $15.00/$35.00.**
◆ **Ken Ceremonie from France, $30.00/$60.00.**
◆ **Three Mode Fantaisie Barbie dolls from France, each $30.00/$40.00.**

Introduced are:
- Peaches'n Cream Barbie and Christie.
- Day-to-Night Barbie and Ken, black Barbie and Ken, and Hispanic Barbie.
- Dance Sensation Barbie Set.
- My First Barbie black and white in a new dress.
- Happy Birthday Barbie Set.
- Dreamtime Barbie with a cute little teddy bear.
- Superstyle Skipper.
- Japanese Barbie.

Foreign dolls:
- Maritim (Sea Lovin') Barbie and Ken from Canada and Europe, Skipper exclusively in Europe. Surprisingly this budget line Barbie is not a cheap doll but a nice Lovin' You Barbie type doll with bend arms.
- Beach Time Barbie, Ken, and Skipper.
- Fruehlingszauber (Springtime Magic) Barbie, a favorite of many collectors. Her outfit only was available one year earlier in the U. S.
- Haar eerste Haar liefste (her first, her most loved) gift set from Holland, including a My First Barbie, case, furniture, and an extra dress.
- Barbie Le Nouveau Theatre de la Mode (or BillyBoy I) Barbie. American born artist BillyBoy in 1985 created the first Barbie mainly aimed at collectors. This Barbie in an edition of 6000 dolls, is only sold in France in cities where a display of his collection and designer gowns is shown.

- **Le Nouveau Theatre De La Mode (BillyBoy I) Barbie (France), $100.00/$200.00.**

- **Haar eerste Haar liefste, My First Barbie gift set from Holland with case, doll, furniture, and extra outfit, $30.00/$70.00.**

1985

◆ **Peaches'n Cream Barbie, $15.00/$25.00.**
◆ **Barbie Lady from Spain, $30.00/$50.00.**
◆ **Peaches'n Cream Barbie, black, $20.00/$30.00.**

◆ **Day-to-Night Barbie, $18.00/$30.00.**
◆ **Day-to-Night Barbie, black, $20.00/$35.00.**
◆ **Day-to-Night Barbie, Hispanic, $20.00/$35.00.**

- **Day-to-Night Ken, black, $20.00/$35.00.**
- **Day-to-Night Ken, $15.00/$25.00.**
- **Fruehlingszauber (Springtime Magic) Barbie from Germany, $80.00/ $120.00.**

- **Dance Sensation Barbie, $30.00/$45.00.**
- **My First Barbie, black, $8.00/$15.00.**
- **May First Barbie, white, $5.00/$10.00.**

◆ **Dreamtime Barbie, $25.00/$40.00.**
◆ **Barbie Dulces Suenos from Spain, $40.00/$60.00.**
◆ **Superstyle (Hot Stuff) Skipper, $10.00/$25.00.**

◆ **Happy Birthday Barbie Party Gift Set, $40.00/$80.00.**
◆ **Japanese Barbie, $90.00/$130.00.**

- ◆ **Beach Time Ken (Europe and Canada), $20.00/$30.00.**
- ◆ **Beach Time Barbie (Europe and Canada), $20.00/$30.00.**
- ◆ **Beach Time Skipper (Europe), $20.00/$30.00.**
- ◆ **Sea Lovin' Barbie (Europe and Canada), $20.00/$35.00.**

- ◆ **Sea Lovin' Ken (Europe and Canada), $15.00/$30.00.**
- ◆ **Sea Lovin' Ken from France, $20.00/$40.00.**
- ◆ **Sea Lovin' Skipper from Spain, $20.00/$45.00.**
- ◆ **Sea Lovin' Skipper (Europe), $15.00/$30.00.**
- ◆ **Sea Lovin' Skipper from France, $20.00/$40.00.**

1986

This year's most unusual dolls are Barbie and the Rockers: Barbie, Diva, Dee Dee, Dana, and their male friend Derek. In Europe these dolls are called Rock Stars and are sold in blue instead of black boxes. Rock Star Lia is a Mexican exclusive.

Also available are:
- Blue Rhapsody Barbie, first in the line of porcelain Barbie dolls.
- Dream Glow Barbie white, black, and Hispanic, Ken white and black.
- Sears 100th Anniversary Barbie.
- Magic Moves Barbie white and black.
- Greek and Peruvian Barbie.
- A new Happy Birthday Barbie: Gift Giving Barbie or Barbie Regalos in Spain.
- Tropical Barbie white, Hispanic, and black, Ken black and white, Miko (called Marina in Europe), and Skipper.
- Astronaut Barbie white and black.
- Music Lovin' Barbie and Ken from Canada (Sears exclusive) and Europe and a matching Skipper, sold in Europe only.
- Barbie Mare from Italy.
- Hiromichi Nakano Barbie, made by Takara from the original Ponytail head mold, only sold in Japan.

- **Porcelain Blue Rhapsody Barbie, $700.00/$850.00.**

- **Rock Star (Rockers) Barbie, $25.00/$40.00.**
- **Rock Star (Rockers) Dee Dee, $30.00/$45.00.**
- **Rockers Dana, $30.00/$45.00.**

- **Lia Rock Star from Mexico, $80.00/$130.00.**
- **Em Ritmo De Rock Barbie from Mexico, $60.00/$90.00.**
- **Rockers Barbie from Venezuela (?), $50.00/$80.00.**

◆ Rock Star (Rockers) Diva, $30.00/$45.00.
◆ Rock Star (Rockers) Derek, $40.00/$65.00.
◆ Barbie Mare from Italy (note the wrist tag!), $20.00/$50.00.

◆ Dream Glow Hispanic Barbie, $20.00/$30.00.
◆ Dream Glow black Barbie, $20.00/$30.00.
◆ Dollar Dream Glow white Barbie, $12.00/$20.00.

- Astronaut Barbie, $50.00/$70.00.
- Astronaut Barbie prototype (gift from Mattel), $150.00.
- Astronaut Barbie, black, $50.00/ $70.00.

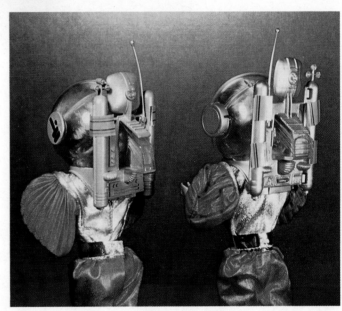

- Closeup of Astronaut Barbie prototype (left) and regular model.

- Magic Moves black Barbie, $30.00/ $45.00.
- Magic Moves white Barbie, $25.00/ $40.00.

1986

- **Dream Glow white Ken, $8.00/$18.00.**
- **Dream Glow black Ken, $20.00/$30.00.**
- **Celebration Barbie, Sears 100th Anniversary Special, $30.00/$55.00.**

- **Greek Barbie, $40.00/$60.00.**
- **Peruvian Barbie, $40.00/$65.00.**
- **Gift Giving Barbie, $15.00/$25.00.**
- **Barbie Regalos from Spain, $30.00/$50.00.**

◆ **Deluxe Tropical Barbie, $15.00/$35.00.**
◆ **Tropical Barbie, $5.00/$12.00.**
◆ **Tropical Barbie from Spain, $15.00/$30.00.**
◆ **Tropical Hispanic Barbie, $10.00/$18.00.**

◆ **Tropical Marina (Europe), $10.00/ $40.00.**
◆ **Tropical Miko, $10.00/$18.00.**
◆ **Tropical black Barbie, $10.00/$18.00.**

◆ **Tropical Ken, $5.00/$10.00.**
◆ **Tropical Ken, black, $10.00/$18.00.**
◆ **Tropical Skipper, $5.00/$10.00.**

◆ **Music Lovin' Ken (Canada and Europe), $25.00/$35.00.**
◆ **Music Lovin' Barbie (Canada and Europe), $25.00/$35.00.**
◆ **Barbie Sport Music from Mexico, $30.00/$45.00.**
◆ **Music Lovin' Skipper (Europe), $30.00/$50.00.**

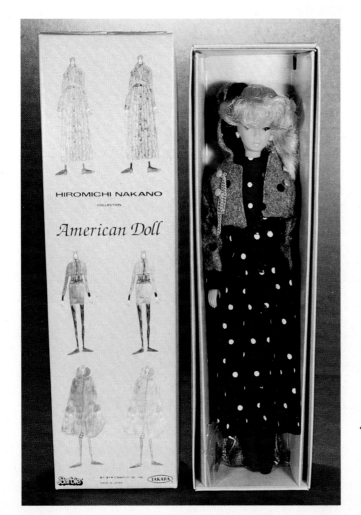

◆ **Hiromichi Nakano American Doll Barbie from Japan, $150.00/$250.00.**

1987

Introduced are:
- Enchanted Evening Porcelain Barbie.
- Feelin' Groovy Barbie (BillyBoy II Barbie).
- Jewel Secrets (Diamant) Barbie and Ken, each white and black, Skipper and their friend Whitney (called Laura in Europe).
- Icelandic and German Barbie dolls.
- My First Barbie Ballerina white, Hispanic, and black.
- Barbie Vacation Sensation, two different play sets.
- Funtime Barbie with a real watch, available in white, black, and different colored outfits.
- Super Hair Barbie black and white.
- Second edition Rocker Barbie, Dee Dee, Diva, Dana, Derek, and new Ken. Again the European versions are called Rock Stars.
- Tennis Stars gift set. Barbie, Ken, and Skipper are sold in Europe by themselves.
- New Fashion Play Barbie dolls on the Canadian and European market. Some have special names: Hostess, Uptown, Pool Side, and Loisirs Barbie.
- Meine erste Barbie set (My First Barbie Set) in a special carrying case with a tape and extra outfit, a German exclusive.
- Takaras P.B. Barbie dolls, made out of the original Ponytail or Twist head mold and sold in only one store in Tokyo, Japan. The clothing is either reproductions of original outfits, some in unusual colors, or an original design.

- **Enchanted Evening Porcelain Barbie, $320.00/ $450.00.**

1987

- ◆ Jewel Secrets white Barbie, $10.00/$20.00.
- ◆ Jewel Secrets black Barbie, $12.00/$25.00.

- ◆ Jewel Secrets white Ken, $10.00/$20.00.
- ◆ Jewel Secrets black Ken, $12.00/$25.00.
- ◆ Jewel Secrets Princess Laura (Europe), $15.00/$50.00 (same doll sold under the name Whitney in the U. S. $15.00/$30.00).

◆ **Barbie Brillantes Secrets from Mexico, $25.00/$45.00.**
◆ **Icelandic Barbie, $50.00/$80.00.**
◆ **German Barbie, $60.00/$90.00.**

◆ **Meine erste Barbie Set gift set from Germany, $15.00/$55.00.**
◆ **Jewel Secrets Skipper, $20.00/$30.00.**

1987

◆ Two Vacation Sensation sets, each $25.00/$40.00.

◆ Ballerina Barbie, white, $5.00/$10.00.
◆ Ballerina Barbie, Hispanic, $10.00/$18.00.
◆ Ballerina Barbie, black, $8.00/$15.00.

◆ Four Funtime Barbie dolls, each $15.00/$25.00.

◆ Funtime Barbie, $15.00/$25.00.
◆ Synchro Barbie from France, $20.00/$40.00.
◆ Super Hair Barbie, black, $15.00/$25.00.
◆ Super Hair Barbie, white, $12.00/$20.00.

1987

- Rock Stars (Rockers) Barbie, $20.00/$35.00.
- Rock Stars (Rockers) Dee Dee, $20.00/$40.00.
- Rock Stars (Rockers) Diva, $20.00/$40.00.

- Rock Stars (Rockers) Dana, $20.00/$40.00.
- Rock Stars (Rockers) Derek, $25.00/$45.00.
- Rock Stars (Rockers) Ken, $20.00/$40.00.

- ◆ **Tennis Stars Barbie and Ken, $30.00/$45.00.**
- ◆ **Tennis Ken (Europe), $15.00/$30.00.**
- ◆ **Tennis Barbie (Europe), $15.00/$30.00.**
- ◆ **Tennis Skipper (Europe), $20.00/$35.00.**

- ◆ **Fashion Play Barbie (Canada and Europe), $8.00 – 15.00.**
- ◆ **Hostess Barbie (Canada), $8.00 – 20.00.**
- ◆ **Uptown Barbie (Canada), $8.00 – 20.00.**
- ◆ **Pool Side Barbie (Canada), $8.00 – 20.00.**
- ◆ **Three Loisirs Barbie dolls (Canada and Europe), $8.00 – 20.00.**

1987

◆ **Feelin' Groovy (BillyBoy II) Barbie,**
   $80.00/$120.00.

◆ **PB Barbie dolls from Japan, each**
   $200.00/$250.00.

◆ **PB Barbie dolls from Japan, each**
   $200.00/$250.00.

◆ **PB Barbie dolls from Japan, each**
   $250.00/$300.00.

◆ **PB Barbie from Japan,** $200.00/$250.00.

◆ **PB Barbie from Japan,** $200.00/$250.00.

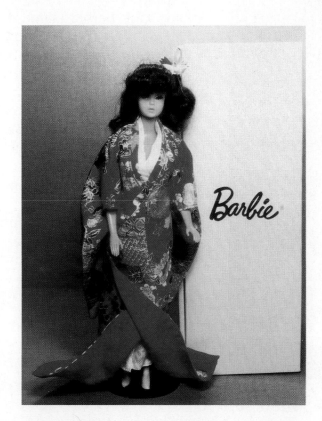

◆ **PB Barbie from Japan, $250.00/** $300.00.

◆ **PB Barbie dolls from Japan, each** $250.00/$300.00.

1988

This year's new dolls are:
- Benefit Performance Porcelain Barbie.
- Perfume Pretty (Bluetenduft) Barbie and Ken, each black and white, and their friend Whitney (called Princess Laura in Europe).
- Sweetheart Skipper.
- Dr. Barbie, Ken, and Nurse Whitney (Laura in Europe).
- Korean and Canadian Barbie dolls.
- Teen Fun Skipper dolls: Cheerleader Teen, Workout Teen, and Party Teen.
- Tropical (Island Fun) Barbie, Teresa, Christie, Miko (Marina), Skipper, Ken black and white.
- Fun-To-Dress Barbie white and black.
- Mardi Gras Barbie.
- Lilac and Lovely Barbie, Sears.
- Skating Star Barbie Calgary Skater with Olympic sticker (Canada only).
- Skating Star Barbie without sticker, available in Europe.
- StarDream Barbie (same doll as Skating Star plus extra skirt), Sears.
- Pink Jubilee Barbie, 25 Years WalMart.
- Party Pink Barbie (same doll as Pink Jubilee, sold in Europe).
- California Barbie, Ken, Teresa, Christie, Midge, and only in Europe Skipper.
- Barbie and the Sensations (BiBops in Europe): Barbie, Belinda, Bibi, Becky, and sold only in France, Bobby.
- My First Barbie Set from Holland.
- Fashion Play Barbie dolls in new outfits (Canada and Europe).

- **Benefit Performance Porcelain Barbie, $480.00/ $550.00.**

- **Perfume Pretty Barbie, $15.00/$30.00.**
- **Perfume Pretty Ken, $15.00/$30.00.**
- **Perfume Pretty Princess Laura (Europe), $20.00/$50.00 (same doll sold in the U. S. under the name Whitney, $20.00/$40.00).**

- **Perfume Pretty black Barbie, $20.00/$35.00.**
- **Perfume Giving black Ken with moustache, $25.00/$40.00.**
- **Sweetheart Skipper, $15.00/$25.00.**

1988

- ◆ Dr. Barbie, $20.00/$35.00.
- ◆ Dr. Ken, $15.00/$30.00.
- ◆ Nurse Laura (Europe), $20.00/$50.00
  (called Whitney in the U.S., $20.00/$40.00).

- ◆ Korean Barbie, $40.00/$50.00.
- ◆ Canadian Barbie, $40.00/$55.00.

◆ BiBops (Sensations) Barbie, $20.00/$35.00.
◆ Sensations Belinda, $20.00/$40.00.
◆ BiBops (Sensations) Bibi, $20.00/$40.00.

◆ BiBops (Sensations) Becky, $20.00/$40.00.
◆ BiBops Bobby from France, $50.00/$80.00.
◆ Mardi Gras Barbie, $60.00/$90.00.

- ◆ Lilac and Lovely Barbie, $30.00/$45.00.
- ◆ Party Pink Barbie (Europe), $30.00/$45.00.
- ◆ Pink Jubilee Barbie, $40.00/$65.00.

- ◆ Club California Barbie with extra tape, $15.00/$25.00 (regular California edition, $10.00/$20.00).
- ◆ Club California Ken, $15.00/$25.00 (regular California edition $10.00/$20.00).
- ◆ California Skipper (Europe), $20.00/$40.00.

◆ **California Dream Teresa, $15.00/$25.00.**
◆ **California Christie, $12.00/$22.00.**
◆ **California Midge, $15.00/$25.00.**

◆ **Skating Star Barbie from Canada, $30.00/$80.00.**
◆ **Skating Star from Switzerland, $30.00/$60.00.**
◆ **Star Dream Barbie, $30.00/$50.00.**

◆ **Three Teen Fun Skipper dolls, each $13.00/$23.00.**

◆ **Tropical (Island Fun) Barbie, $5.00/$10.00.**
◆ **Island Fun Teresa, $8.00/$15.00.**
◆ **Island Fun Christie, $8.00/$15.00.**
◆ **Tropical (Island Fun) Marina (Europe), $8.00/$25.00.**
◆ **Island Fun Miko, $8.00/$15.00.**

- ◆ **Tropical (Island Fun) Skipper, $5.00/$10.00.**
- ◆ **Tropical (Island Fun) Ken, $5.00/$10.00.**
- ◆ **Island Fun Steven, $8.00/$15.00.**
- ◆ **My First Barbie Set from Holland, $20.00/$35.00.**

- ◆ **Five Fashion Play (Mode) Barbie (Europe and Canada), each $8.00/$15.00.**
- ◆ **Fun-To-Dress Barbie, black, $8.00/$15.00.**
- ◆ **Fun-To-Dress Barbie, white, $5.00/$10.00.**

Barbie Through the Years

1989

Little girls and collectors can choose from:

- Barbie Wedding Party Porcelain Barbie, which is hard to find. Rumor says that the mold form broke before the edition was finished.
- First in series and a collector's favorite: Happy Holidays Barbie. In Europe Happy Holiday Barbie dolls used to be sold one year behind. So in 1990, when the doll became rare in the U.S. a lot of European Happy Holidays Barbie dolls were brought over. Still today the prices for these European dolls are lower than for the U.S. ones. The dolls and outfits are the same except for a different hair ornament and the box.
- Super Star Barbie and Ken, black and white.

- **Wedding Day Porcelain Barbie, $500.00/$600.00.**

- Cool Times Barbie, Christie, Midge, Teresa, and Ken.
- Animal Lovin' (Safari) Barbie, black Barbie, Nikki, and Ken.
- Beach Blast (Sun Magic) Barbie, Teresa, Christie, Miko (Marina), Ken, black Ken, Skipper.
- Style Magic Barbie, Christie, and Whitney.
- Super Style Barbie from Europe is the same doll as Style Magic, but comes in a slightly different dress. Super Style Skipper (European exclusive).
- Feeling Fun Barbie, called Jeans Barbie in Europe.
- Barbie doll's cousin Jazzie and friends: Jazzie Teen Dance, High School, Teen Looks (Workout, Cheerleader, Swim Suit), Stacie, Chelsie, and Dude.
- Homecoming Queen Skipper, white and black.
- Teen Time Skipper and Courtney.
- My First Ken.
- Gift Giving Barbie.
- Ma Premiere Barbie Miniclub from France.
- Mexican and Russian Barbie dolls.
- Golden Greetings Barbie, FAO Schwarz.
- Show'N Ride Set.

- Frills and Fantasy, WalMart.
- Barbie Chick (Spanish exclusive).
- From Europe: Garden Party Barbie.
  - Two new Fashion Play Barbie dolls.
  - St. Tropez Barbie.
  - 1+2 Gift set with two extra outfits.

◆ **Happy Holidays (I) Barbie dolls. Left, European version, $200.00/$350.00. Right, U.S. version, $350.00/$650.00.**

◆ **Super Star Barbie, $15.00/$25.00.**
◆ **Super Star Ken, $15.00/$25.00.**
◆ **Super Star black Ken, $20.00/$30.00.**

1989

- ◆ **Super Star black Barbie, $20.00/$30.00.**
- ◆ **My First Ken, $5.00/$10.00.**
- ◆ **My First Barbie Miniclub (France), $5.00/$25.00 (U. S. version, $5.00/$10.00).**
- ◆ **Gift Giving Barbie, $12.00/$23.00.**

- ◆ **Safari Barbie, $10.00/$20.00.**
- ◆ **Animal Lovin' (Safari) black Barbie, $15.00/$25.00.**
- ◆ **Animal Lovin' (Safari) Nikki, $15.00/$30.00.**
- ◆ **Safari Ken, $10.00/$20.00.**

- ◆ **Cool Times Barbie,** $10.00/$20.00.
- ◆ **Cool Times Christie,** $15.00/$25.00.
- ◆ **Cool Times Midge,** $15.00/$25.00.

- ◆ **Cool Times Teresa,** $15.00/$25.00.
- ◆ **Cool Times Ken,** $10.00/$20.00.
- ◆ **Show'N Ride Barbie,** $30.00/$45.00.

1989

- ◆ Sun Magic (Beach Blast) Barbie, $5.00/$10.00.
- ◆ Beach Blast Teresa, $8.00/$15.00.
- ◆ Beach Blast Christie, $8.00/$15.00.
- ◆ Beach Blast Miko, $8.00/$15.00.
- ◆ Beach Blast Marina (Europe), $8.00/$25.00.

- ◆ Sun Magic (Beach Blast) Skipper, $5.00/$10.00.
- ◆ Sun Magic (Beach Blast) Ken, $5.00/$10.00.
- ◆ Beach Blast Steven, $8.00/$15.00.
- ◆ Frills and Fantasy Barbie, $20.00/$30.00.

- ◆ **Garden Party Barbie (Europe), $20.00/$35.00.**
- ◆ **Golden Greetings Barbie, $100.00/$200.00.**

- ◆ **Style Magic Barbie, $10.00/$20.00.**
- ◆ **Super Style Barbie (Europe), $15.00/$30.00.**
- ◆ **Super Style Skipper (Europe), $20.00/$40.00.**

- ◆ **Style Magic Whitney, $15.00/$25.00.**
- ◆ **Style Magic Christie, $10.00/$25.00.**
- ◆ **Barbie Jeans (Europe), $10.00/$20.00.**
- ◆ **Feeling Fun Barbie, $10.00/$15.00.**

- ◆ **Mexican Barbie, $30.00/$45.00.**
- ◆ **Russian Barbie, $30.00/$45.00.**
- ◆ **1 + 2 Barbie set from Europe, $12.00/$30.00.**

- ◆ **Teen Time Skipper, $9.00/$18.00.**
- ◆ **Teen Time Courtney, $10.00/$20.00.**
- ◆ **St. Tropez Barbie (Europe), $8.00/$15.00.**
- ◆ **Barbie Chic from Spain, $20.00/$35.00.**

- ◆ **Homecoming Queen Skipper, black, $10.00/$20.00.**
- ◆ **Teen Romance (Homecoming Queen) Skipper, white, $9.00/$18.00.**
- ◆ **Two Fashion Play Barbie dolls (Europe), each $8.00/$15.00.**

1989

- ◆ Teen Dance Jazzie, $15.00/$30.00.
- ◆ High School Jazzie, $12.00/$25.00.
- ◆ Teen Looks Workout Jazzie, $10.00/$20.00.
- ◆ Teen Looks Cheerleader Jazzie, $10.00/$20.00.

- ◆ Teen Looks Swim Suit Jazzie, $10.00/$20.00.
- ◆ High School Stacie, $20.00/$35.00.
- ◆ High School Chelsie, $20.00/$35.00.
- ◆ High School Dude, $20.00/$40.00.

Foreign Dolls

from the 1980s

Many foreign dolls have no date on their box so it is hard to find out when exactly they were on the market.

The Japanese toy manufacturer Takara started to produce unique Barbie dolls under license from Mattel in 1982. In 1986 the license went to Ma-ba, a company that was controlled partly by Mattel, partly by another Japanese toy manufacturer, Bandai (Ma-ba — Ma for Mattel and Ba for Bandai). These new Barbie dolls are slightly different from the Takara Barbie dolls. They have smaller heads and a different look. Takara went on producing dolls of the same type as before. As they could no longer sell the dolls as Barbie dolls they changed the doll's name to Jenny.

From 1990 on (for only a short few years) Bandai alone got the license to produce Barbie dolls.

Now, to the loss of children and collectors alike, the special productions for the Japanese market stopped and only the regular line of Barbie dolls is offered in Japan.

 ◆ **Takara Mink Barbie (with a jacket out of real mink!),** **$350.00/$450.00.**

Takara Barbie dolls:
- ◆ **Barbie, $40.00/$60.00.**
- ◆ **Dream Barbie, $50.00/$70.00.**
- ◆ **Exelina Barbie, $60.00/$100.00.**
- ◆ **Wedding Barbie, $50.00/$70.00.**

Takara dolls:
- ◆ Ellie, Barbie doll's friend, $60.00/$100.00.
- ◆ Floral Land Flora (doll produced after Takara lost the license, so not part of the Barbie line), $30.00/$40.00.
- ◆ Flora, Barbie doll's friend, $60.00/$100.00.
- ◆ Ken, $60.00/$100.00.

- **Ma-ba Kimono Barbie, $50.00/$80.00.**
- **Two Takara Kimono Barbie dolls, each $60.00/$100.00.**
- **Ma-ba kimono, $40.00/$50.00.**

- **Transitional Barbie/Jenny. Jenny box but Barbie outfit, $60.00/$100.00.**
- **Bandai Barbie Lesson, $45.00/$70.00.**
- **Takara Kiss Barbie, $50.00/$70.00.**

Foreign Dolls
from the
1980s

◆ **Kansai designer Barbie from Takara, $70.00/$140.00.**

◆ **Ma-ba Crystal Queen Barbie, $50.00/$80.00.**
◆ **Ma-ba Beautiful Bride Barbie, $50.00/$80.00.**
◆ **Ma-ba Princess Bride Barbie, $50.00/$80.00.**
◆ **Takara Fantasy Barbie, $60.00/$100.00.**

◆ **Ma-ba Flower Barbie, $40.00/$60.00.**
◆ **Two Ma-ba Ken dolls, each $80.00/$100.00.**
◆ **Ma-ba Beautiful Barbie, $40.00/$60.00.**

Ma-ba Barbie dolls:
◆ **Two wind up musical (stand) Barbie dolls, $90.00/$120.00.**
◆ **Diamond Dream Barbie, $50.00/$80.00.**

Foreign Dolls
from the
1980s

◆ **Ma-ba Glamorous U.S. Barbie
   dolls, each $50.00/$100.00.**

Ma-ba dolls:
   ◆ **Noel and Sophie, Barbie doll's friends, each
      $80.00/$100.00.**
   ◆ **Stefanie, Barbie doll's teacher, $90.00/$110.00.**
   ◆ **Barbie Crepe Shop, $40.00/$60.00.**

Bandai Barbie dolls:
- ◆ **Star Princess Barbie, $50.00/$80.00.**
- ◆ **Happy Bridal Barbie, each $50.00/$80.00.**

- ◆ **Ma-ba gift set, $60.00/$100.00.**

◆ **Japanese set, late 1970s, $50.00/$130.00.**

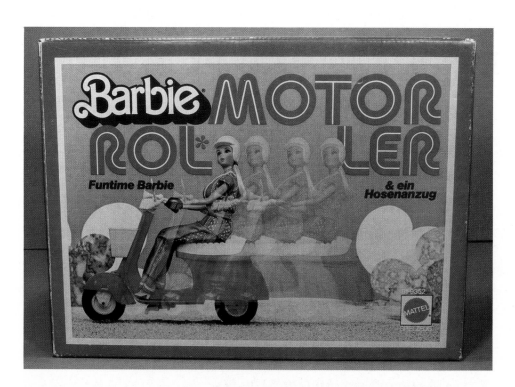

◆ **Barbie Motor Roller set from Germany, includes a Funtime Barbie in box, the pictured green outfit, and the vehicle, No. 91-9352, 1979, $70.00/$300.00.**

◆ **Barbie from Korea, $50.00/$80.00.**

◆ **Barbie dolls from Korea, $50.00/$80.00 each.**

Foreign Dolls
from the
1980s

◆ Barbie and her friend Valerie
from Mexico, late 70s, Barbie,
$90.00/$130.00; Valerie,
$150.00/$250.00.

◆ Friendship I (Berlin
Wall) Barbie. This doll
was sold only in East
Germany after the fall
of the Berlin Wall to
celebrate this event,
1990, $40.00/$60.00.

◆ Greek Barbie with a
candle for girls to hold
through religious pro-
cessions. Note the
crudely made skirt.
Barbie couldn't attend
in a bathing suit.
$70.00/$120.00.

◆ **Mexican Barbie Ciclista,**
$150.00/$200.00.

◆ **Western Barbie set and 4 estaciones set both from Mexico, each**
$60.00/$90.00.

◆ **Sensación Barbie set and 5 Aniversario set both from Mexico, each $60.00/$90.00.**

◆ **Dazzling Pretty Barbie from Philippines, $30.00 – 50.00.**
◆ **Viky from Mexico, $120.00/$200.00.**
◆ **Barbie from Mexico, $70.00/$100.00.**

Venezuelan Barbie dolls:
- ◆ **Spring Time Barbie, $60.00/$90.00.**
- ◆ **Blue Magic Barbie, $50.00/$80.00.**
- ◆ **Llanera Barbie, $80.00/$130.00.**

- ◆ **Barbie 10th Aniversario from Spain, $90.00/$150.00.**
- ◆ **Barbie 5th Aniversario from Portugal, $50.00/$90.00.**

Barbie

Variations are outfits in different fabric and/or colors but with the same stock number and name. Some variations were planned by Mattel as a fashionable change of outfits or to use up fabric left over from other garments.

Other variations happened more by accident when Mattel ran out of material during production. When only a few more outfits had to be finished it was easier to use a fabric that was on hand. When a greater amount of fabric was missing it was re-ordered and often turned out to be slightly different.

◆ **Commuter Set, #916, 1959, (Lilli, No. 3 Barbie). Notice the hats in three different colors (pink, fuchsia, and red) and "R" and "TM" hatboxes, $400.00 each.**

From the early 1960s on, Mattel offered special outfits in foreign countries to complement the different tastes and lifestyles. Some of these special outfits resemble regular outfits but have different stock numbers and names. Often it is unknown whether an unusual garment found in a foreign country is a variation of a regular outfits, a foreign special, or a prototype.

There are not only hundreds but thousands of variations, prototypes, and foreign outfits out there. Every day new ones are found. Collecting them is never-ending fun.

The prices given are for mint and complete outfits (even if only one of several similar outfits is shown with all the accessories). For doll prices see doll section. If a boxed garment is pictured, both the price for a mint and a boxed item are given. If an outfit doesn't have an English name, the German name is given. In the Tutti section also some regular edition outfits are shown.

◆ **Apple Print Sheath, #917, 1959, (Two Bubble Cut Barbie dolls), $50.00, left; $60.00, right.**

◆ **Busy Gal, #981, 1960, (Two No. 3 Barbie dolls), $150.00, $200.00.**
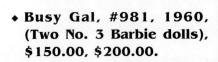

◆ Silk Sheath, pak, 1962, (three Midge dolls, Swirl Ponytail Barbie, Fashion Queen Barbie, Ponytail Barbie) each $35.00 except red and black version (not shown) $100.00 each.

◆ Sheath with Gold Buttons, pak 1962, floral version 1964, (Ponytail, Bubble Cut, Fashion Queen, and Swirl Ponytail Barbie dolls), floral version $40.00, others $25.00 each.

♦ Enchanted Evening, #983, 1960,
(Two No. 3 Barbie dolls), $150.00,
right Japanese version, #B983,
1960, $450.00.

♦ Pajama Party, pak, 1962 (Swirl
Ponytail Barbie, Midge, Fashion
Queen Barbie), $20.00 each.
♦ Back: Pajama Party, #1601,
1964, $20.00/$60.00.
♦ Suzy Goose Skipper bed,
$80.00.

◆ After 5, #934, 1962 (Midge, Bubble Cut Barbie), faille fabric $50.00, polished cotton $70.00.

◆ Dinner At Eight, #946, 1963, (Ponytail Barbie) with unusual light orange long gloves (found in Germany), $150.00.

◆ Campus Belle, pak, 1964 (Bubble Cut and Swirl Ponytail Barbie dolls), each $90.00.

- Cinderella #872, 1964, (Fashion Queen, Swirl Ponytail, and American Girl Barbie dolls), notice the variations of the rich dress, each set $180.00.
- The Prince, #772, 1964, (first Ken), notice the rare high heel glass slipper and the regular version, $130.00 (add $30.00 if it comes with the rare slipper).

- Campus Sweetheart, #1616, 1965, (two Bubble Cut Sidepart Barbie dolls), left $400.00, right Japanese version, $500.00.

◆ Midnight Blue, #1617, 1965, (American Girl and Bubble Cut Barbie dolls) rare steel blue version $500.00, intense blue version $300.00.

◆ It's Cold Outside, #819, 1964, (Fashion Queen Barbie, Midge) brown $40.00, red $60.00.

◆ Saturday Matinee, #1615, 1965, (Swirl Ponytail Barbie dolls), left with light brown fur found in Germany, $400.00, right regular outfit, $320.00.

◆ Belle Dress, pak, 1962 (Fashion Queen, Ponytail, Bubble Cut Barbie dolls), each $15.00.

◆ In the Swim, pak, 1964, (three Bubble Cut Barbie dolls), each $45.00.

◆ **Red Delight, pak, 1966 (Bubble Cut Barbie), $90.00.**
◆ **Matinee Fashion, #1640, 1965, slightly different fabric than the pak, $300.00/$400.00.**

Pak items:

◆ **Tops: Tailored Tops, 1966, each $30.00.**
◆ **Scoop Neck Playsuit, 1962, $5.00.**
◆ **Plain Blouse, 1962, $5.00.**

◆ **Skirts: Pert Skirts, 1966, each $40.00. (Swirl Ponytail, Bubble Cut, and Ponytail Barbie dolls and Molded Hair Midge)**

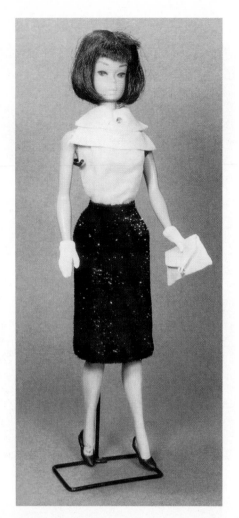

◆ **Atelier Fest, #1680, 1967, European exclusive, (American Girl Barbie), $1,300.00.**

◆ **Lunch Date, pak, 1966, (two Bubble Cut Barbie dolls), left Knit Hit fabric (#1621, 1965) $80.00, right Poodle Parade fabric (#1643, 1965) $90.00.**

◆ **Country Club Dance, #1627, 1965 (two Swirl Ponytail Barbie dolls), crepe or knit fabric, each $160.00.**

◆ Reception Line, #1654, 1966, (two Bubble Cut Barbie dolls), left unusual light blue from Germany (not faded), $300.00, right $230.00.

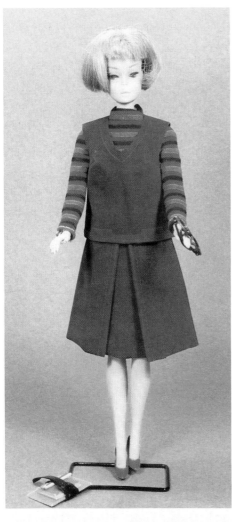

◆ Sorbonne, #1679, 1967, sold only in Europe (American Girl Barbie), $1,200.00.

◆ Gala Abend, #1671, 1967, sold in Europe and Japan, missing paper booklet (Sidepart American Girl Barbie), $1,500.00.

◆ **Pink Moonbeams, #1694, 1967
(Bubble Cut Barbie dolls), pink
$75.00, light pink $65.00.**

◆ **Formal Occasion #1697, 1967 (rare plat-
inum Sidepart Bubble Cut Barbie, Bubble
Cut Barbie), left unusual version (the lace
is from Red Fantastic, a Sears exclusive
from 1967) found in Germany, $500.00,
right $250.00.**

♦ Fashion Shiner, #1691, 1967
(Sidepart Bubble Cut Barbie
and Swirl Ponytail Barbie), left
regular shiny version $85.00,
right dull fabric $100.00.

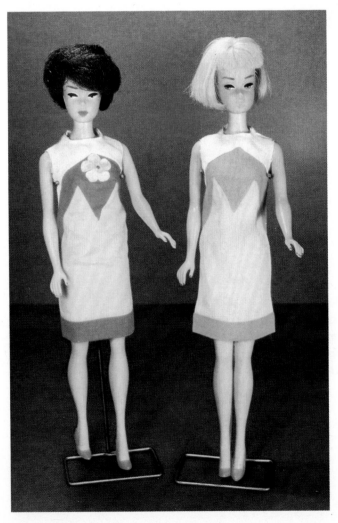

♦ Tropicana #1460, 1967 (Bubble Cut
and American Girl Barbie dolls), left
$60.00, right $80.00 (flower missing).

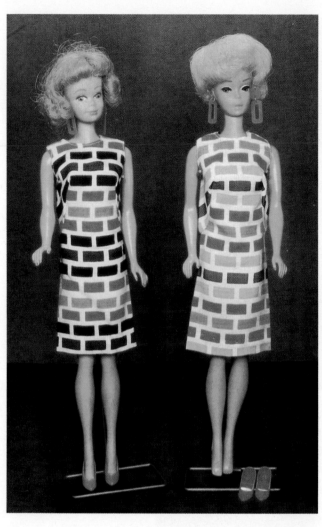

◆ Print Aplenty, #1686, 1967 (Midge, Bubble Cut Barbie), left $85.00, right $95.00.

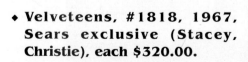

◆ Velveteens, #1818, 1967, Sears exclusive (Stacey, Christie), each $320.00.

♦ Best Bow, pak, 1967, made from the same pattern as Beau Time (#1651, 1966) (Bubble Cut, Swirl Ponytail, and Sidepart Bubble Cut Barbie dolls), 3 of about 10 known variations, most came with a bow (material from Gay Parisienne #964, 1958, and Allan doll's beach jacket), each $90.00.

♦ Dressed Up, pak, 1967, regardless of the color of the dress this outfit seems to have always come with green high heel shoes (Twist Barbie) (fabric from Golden Glory #1645, 1965, Fashion Queen Barbie original outfit, and others), $90.00/$130.00.

◆ **Fab Fur, #1493, 1968 (Stacey, Christie), left $100.00, right unusual variation (Francie Fur-Out, #1262, 1966 fabric), $350.00.**

Japanese Mod outfits:
◆ **Left: Twist Barbie in the outfit she was sold in (dressed doll) $250.00 with doll.**
◆ **Middle: unknown stock number (Hair Fair Head Barbie), $180.00.**
◆ **Right: dress only #21002618 (Talking Barbie), $130.00.**

◆ **Candlelight Capers, #1753, 1969, (Julia dolls), left $65.00, right with unusual top $140.00.**

◆ **Dreamy Pink, #1857, 1969, (Standard Barbie), light pink $30.00/$70.00, dark pink $40.00.**

◆ **Terrific Twosome, pak, 1969 (Busy Barbie, Hair Fair Head Barbie),
the fabric of the very right top was also used for a Japanese special pak sheath. Skippin' Rope, #3604, 1966 material was used for
the red skirt. $90.00 for the boxed set, $15.00 for each item.**

◆ **Three variations of Brr Furr, #1752, 1969, (Julia), left $130.00/$180.00,
middle $140.00, right $55.00/$90.00.**

- **Dotted outfits: Sunshiner, pak, 1969 (same fabric as Studio Tour #1690, 1967) (Miss America, Stacey, Fair Hair Head Barbie), $15.00 each.**
- **Middle: Swirly-Cue #1822, 1968 (Twist Barbie), $60.00.**
- **Yellow outfit with flowers: Sunshine, Pak, 1969, out of Travel Together material (#1688, 1967), $15.00.**

- **Great Coat, #1459, 1970 (rare redheaded Twist Barbie), $25.00.**
- **On the hanger: Japanese version, #14591, $80.00. (Purse of the same material belongs to outfit #3359, 1972.)**

• **Fur Sighted, #1796, 1970, (Standard Barbie, Hair Fair Head Barbie), red ensemble $70.00, orange $90.00.**

• **Left: Soft N'Snug, pak, 1970, (Talking Barbie) $8.00.**
• **Middle and right: Scuba-Dos, #1788, 1970 (Twist Barbie) middle $35.00/ $55.00, right with swim suit out of a Twiggy outfit material (Twigster, #1727, 1968), $55.00.**

♦ **Left: Ruffles N'Swirls, #1783, 1970
(Hair Fair Head Barbie), $40.00.**
♦ **Right: Walking Pretty, pak, 1970
(Twist Barbie), $35.00.**

♦ **Soft Snug, pak, 1970,
each $30.00/$50.00.**

◆ **Sharp Shift, pak, 1970 (Standard Barbie, Christie, Stacey, Hair Fair Head Barbie):** Middle outfit is made from Clear Out (#1281, 1967) material. Packaged outfit is from same fabric as Togetherness (#1842, 1968). Right dress made out of Twiggy doll's original outfit material. Three left outfits $40.00 each. Two right dresses $20.00/$50.00 each.

◆ **Cool 'N Casual, pak, 1970 (Christie, Two Twist Barbie dolls, PJ),** fabric used from: Sun Spots (#1277, 1967), Dancing Stripes (#1843, 1966), Junior Designer (#1620, 1965), It's a Date (#1251, 1966), Little Red Riding Hood (#880, 1964), and special pak fabric, each $30.00.

◆ **Barbie Fashion Bouquet, pak, Sears exclusive, 1970 (Talking Barbie, Hair Fair Head Barbie, Twist Barbie), fabric from: Shoppin' Spree (#1261, 1966), Talking Barbie Gift Set (1970), Pink Sparkle (#1440, 1967), each $35.00.**

◆ **Barbie Fashion Bouquet, pak, Sears Exclusive, 1970 (Walk Lively Barbie and Miss America), left $35.00, right $65.00.**

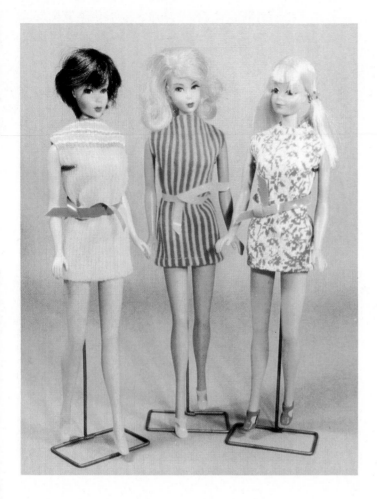

◆ Sundress from Sears Barbie Glamour Group, 1970 (Hair Fair Head Barbie, Twist Barbie, PJ), fabric on left used from Twiggy-Dos material (#1725, 1968), fabric in center from Twigster (#1727, 1968), each $25.00.

◆ Sears Barbie Glamour Group, 1970 (Twist and Hair Fair Head Barbie) each $40.00.

◆ Sears Barbie Glamour Group, 1970 (Live Action PJ and Christie), each $50.00.

◆ Sears Barbie Glamour Group, 1970 (Twist Barbie, Living Barbie, PJ, and Barbie with Growin' Pretty Hair), top four coats each $20.00, coats on the bottom each $35.00.

♦ Suede 'N Fur, #3491, 1971 (Hair Fair Head Barbie, Stacey), left regular edition $85.00, right $150.00.

♦ Left: Wild Things, #3439, 1971 (Miss America), $50.00.
♦ Right: St. Moritz, #7978, 1974, from Europe, missing hat and purse (Malibu Barbie), $100.00.

◆ **The Dream Team, #3427, 1971
(Live Action Barbie and
Christie) white and off-white
versions each $35.00 (book and
scale belong to other outfits).**

◆ **Standing: All American Girl,
#3337, 1972 (Hair Fair Head Bar-
bie dolls), $45.00.**
◆ **Sitting: unknown top, perhaps a
prototype, $70.00.**

◆ **Flying Colors, #3492, 1972 (Hair Fair Head Barbie dolls), each $85.00.**

◆ **Dirndl-Look, #3355, 1972 (Christie and Steffie), dark version $15.00, light outfit $35.00.**

♦ Sleepy Set, #3487, 1972 (Live Action PJ, Christie, Twist Barbie, Living Barbie), each $50.00; except second coat from left which is made out of Midi Duet fabric (#3451, 1971), $100.00.

♦ Blumenreigen, #8620, 1972 (Sweet 16 and Malibu Barbie dolls), left dress is missing the red button, each $5.00.

◆ Hosenanzug, #3208, 1973
(Malibu Barbie and PJ), left
$50.00, right $15.00.

◆ Live Action Ken and a version of
Modisch Chic, #8680, 1974
(Living Barbie), $60.00.

♦ Talking PJ in her original outfit
and two other versions of Modisch
Chic, #8680, 1974 (Twist Barbie
dolls), each $60.00.

♦ Walk Lively Steffie in her original jump-
suit and an unknown outfit out of the
same material. It has a slightly different
cut from Modisch Chic, #8680, 1974
(Talking Barbie), $65.00.

◆ **Right: Living Barbie in her original outfit.**
◆ **Center: Best Buy, #1900, 1980, $60.00/$90.00.**
◆ **Left: an unknown dress out of the same material (Living Barbie), $60.00.**

◆ **Spitzen Elegance, #8688, 1974 (Barbie Plus 3, Malibu Christie), left $10.00, right $25.00.**

◆ **Three versions of Aktuelle Hosenmode, #8685, 1973 (Malibu Barbie dolls and Malibu PJ), felt or knitted vest, each $12.00. Right outfit with pants out of Best Buy #3343 material, 1973, $45.00.**

◆ **Right: Warm Verpackt, #8197, 1974, German exclusive (Twist Barbie), $70.00.**
◆ **Left: The similar Anti-Freezers, #1464, 1970, $45.00/$120.00.**

◆ **Ledermantel mit Pelz, #7977, 1974, found in Germany (Malibu Barbie dolls), each $60.00.**

From Germany:
◆ **Left, Modisch Kombiniert, #7979, $60.00/$100.00.**
◆ **Right, Grosse Mode, #7178, $70.00/$110.00.**

From Germany:
- **Left, #9422 (name unknown), 1976, $60.00/$100.00.**
- **Right, Atelier Fest, #2256, 1979, $90.00/$150.00.**

- **Growing Up Skipper Fashion, #9024, 1975, and a matching European Barbie outfit Freizeitmode, #7178, 1975 (Yellowstone Kelley), $60.00.**

◆ **Im Urlaub, #7210, 1975 (#8588 Barbie and Malibu Barbie), yellow ensemble $45.00, blue $20.00.**

◆ **Bunt gebluemt, #7204, 1975 (Malibu Barbie and PJ), left regular version $10.00, right variation $25.00.**

♦ German Masquerade, #9472, 1977 (Twist Barbie and Hair Fair Head Barbie), left-over fabric from Truly Scrumptious outfit was used, $250.00/$350.00.

♦ Romantic-Look, #7208, 1975 (Quick Curl Cara) (the regular version is cream with some red flowers) fabric from Party Kleid #7205, 1975, $30.00.

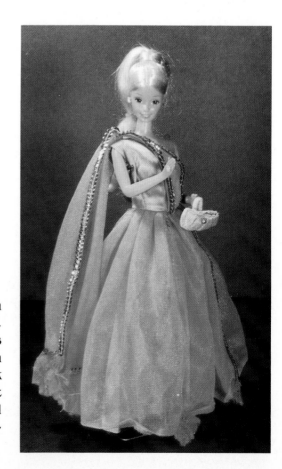

♦ Walzermelodie from Germany, #9471, 1977, $100.00. This outfit was sold in the U.S. in pink (#9972 department store special) and white (#9836 Super-Star fashion).

◆ Elegance, #9469, 1977 (Super-Star Barbie and Hispanic Barbie), left European version $80.00, right $30.00.

◆ Chick kombiniert from Germany, #2255, 1978, $40.00/$70.00.

◆ Reit-Dess, #9423, 1978, Europe (Tracy and Sweet Roses PJ with shortened hair), the outfit came with pants, shirt, skirt, and one jacket, $50.00.

◆ Super Star Hawaiian Barbie in her original outfit from Germany, 1978, and Best Buy #1360, 1979, from same material, $30.00/$45.00. (For regular version see picture on the package.)

◆ Kissing Christie, 1979, with
Bargain Fashion, #5198,
1979, $15.00/$25.00.

◆ Schulball, #2773, 1979 (Rocker
II and Cool Time Barbie dolls),
left $3.00, right $8.00.

◆ Fashion Collectibles, #1904, 1981
(see regular fabric pictured on the
package), $15.00/$25.00.

◆ Best Buy from 1980: two outfits for Ken, #1380; 3 Barbie dresses,
#1351; Skipper outfit, #2923 (Malibu Ken, Hawaiian Barbie, Music Lovin'
Barbie from Spain, Tennis Ken, and Tennis Skipper); packaged dress,
$15.00/$25.00; other Barbie dresses, $3.00; Skipper outfit, $10.00; Ken
outfits, $8.00.

♦ **European genuine fur outfits, #3676, 1980, each $60.00/$100.00.**

♦ **European genuine fur outfits, #3676, 1980, each $60.00/$100.00.**

◆ **European genuine leather outfits, #2901, 1980, each $50.00/ $90.00.**

◆ **European genuine leather outfits, #2901, 1980, each $50.00/ $90.00.**

◆ **Italian Alta Moda outfits from 1980, stock numbers unknown, $20.00/$40.00 each.**

◆ **Italian outfits from 1980, stock numbers unknown, Fai Da Te kit for making leather outfits, $40.00/$90.00; leather dress, $50.00/$90.00.**

• **Italian dresses, 1987, right box has no number; left box #8380, each $20.00/$35.00.**

• **Outfits for Chantal Goya from France, #8963, each $20.00/$40.00.**

◆ Opal, #1359, 1980 (Midge,
Grandma Heart), each $8.00.

◆ Music Lovin' Barbie, 1986, and
pak outfit, 1989, (Hispanic
Barbie), $5.00/$10.00.

La Super Estrella Mundial

Barbie

• **Spanish Barbie outfit, #2301, 1983, $30.00/$50.00.**

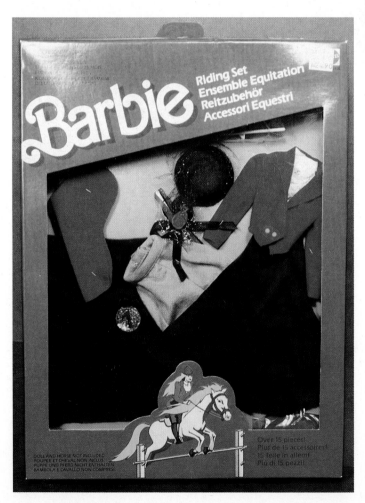

• **Riding Set from Germany (available in the U.S. without the hat), #5400, $25.00/$35.00.**

◆ **Astro Fashion, #2738, 1986, $30.00/$50.00. Prototype outfit
(gift from Mattel together with doll and box), $200.00.**

◆ **Astro Fashion, #2739, 1986, $30.00/$50.00. Prototype outfit (gift
from Mattel together with dolls), $180.00.**

◆ **Left: Ready to Wear fashion, #3313, 1987, $15.00/$30.00.**
◆ **Center and right: #1082, 1989, each $5.00/$10.00.**

◆ **#1063, 1984, each $3.00/$5.00.**

The following outfits belong to the Haute Couture line from Europe.

◆ #3247, 1986, $35.00/$50.00.

◆ #5846, 1983, $50.00/$80.00.

◆ #5841 and #5844, 1984, $40.00/$60.00 each.

◆ #4873 and #5842, 1984, 1985, $40.00/$60.00 each.

◆ **#4874 and #5843, 1984, 1985, $40.00/$60.00 each.**

◆ **#7201 and #5845, 1984, 1985, $40.00/$60.00 each.**

◆ **#7202 and #7204, 1984, $50.00/$70.00 each.**

◆ #9149 and #9150, 1985, $35.00/$50.00 each.

◆ #9151 and #9148, 1985, $35.00/$50.00 each.

◆ #3248, 1986, $35.00/$50.00 each.

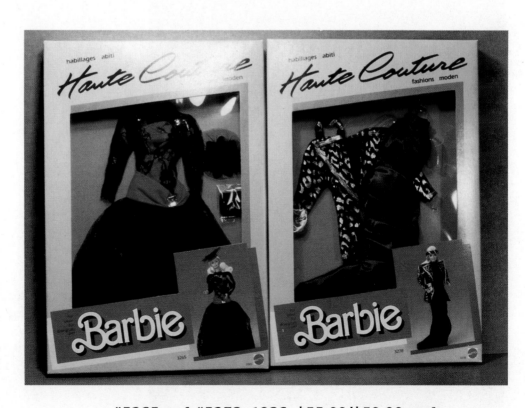

◆ #3265 and #3278, 1986, $35.00/$50.00 each.

Ken

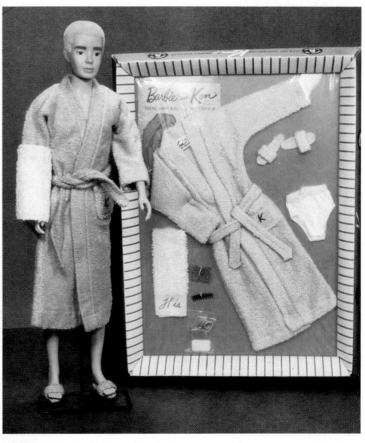

♦ **Terry Togs, #784, 1961 (First Ken), light blue version $30.00/$80.00; darker blue version $50.00.**

♦ **Corduroy jacket and slacks, paks, 1962 (Bendable Leg Allen, First Ken), each piece $10.00/$30.00. Jacket and slacks were also sold together as Campus Corduroy, #1410, 1964, $30.00/$90.00.**

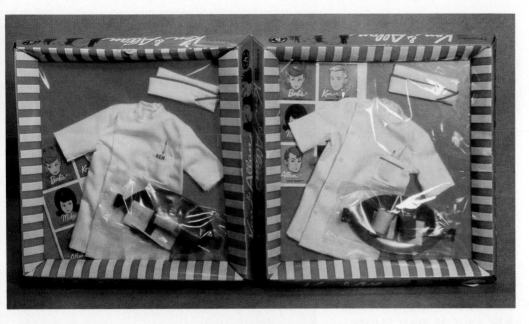

◆ **Fountain Boy, #1407, 1964 (note the different pockets), $80.00/ $130.00.**

◆ **Casual All Star Wardrobe Set from Sears, 1970 (Bendable Leg II Ken dolls), each piece $10.00.**

♦ **Tops: Sun Fun, pak, 1970 (Bendable Leg II Ken dolls), $15.00.**

♦ **Shore Lines, #1435, 1970 (Partytime and Talking Ken dolls), boxed unusual version pants (same material as used for Sun Fun pak), $40.00/$90.00; regular version $30.00.**

• Sea Scene, #1449, 1971 (Talking Ken), each $35.00/$90.00. Notice the different fabric of the suits (woven/printed), white top is a replacement.

• Red, White, and Wild, #1829, 1972 (Funtime Ken), left version $35.00, right $50.00/$80.00.

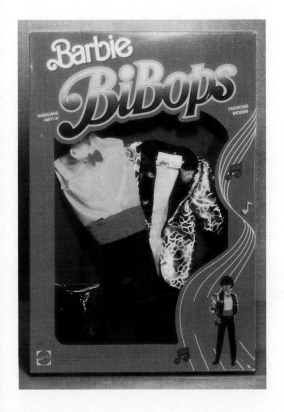

• Bobby BiBops (Sensations) fashion from France, #4990, 1988, $25.00/$45.00.

Francie

- **Japanese Kimono, #2208, 1967 (Twist Francie dolls), shoes are replaced, $500.00 each.**
- **Background: Teen Dream Bedroom, 1971.**

- **Pleat Neat, pak, 1967 (Bendable Leg and Twist Francie dolls), came with pointy-toed yellow shoes (was also available in pink and possibly red), each $60.00.**

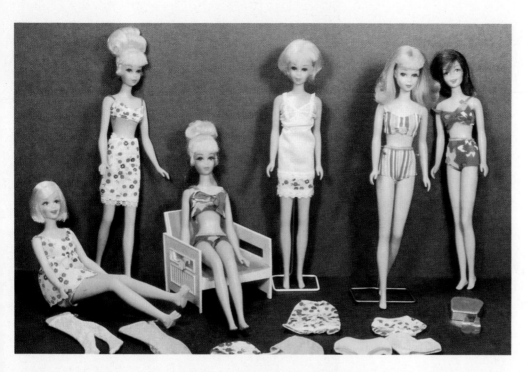

- Doll seated in chair and two on right: Get Readies, pak, 1968 (Francie With Growin' Pretty Hair, Bendable Leg Francie, Casey), each $45.00.
- Left: Pretty Power nightie, #1512, 1970 Sears (Casey), $15.00.
- Left and middle standing: First Things First, #1252, 1966 (Francie With Growin' Pretty Hair and Hair Happenin's Francie), $35.00.
- Bottom: Most are Undies, pak, 1967, $35.00.

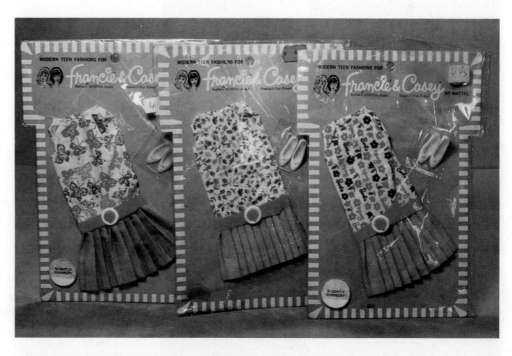

- Slightly Summery, pak, 1968, material from: Brunch Time (#1638, 1965), Right in Style (#1942, 1967), Barbie Learns to Cook (#1634, 1965), and other outfits, each $65.00/$100.00.

◆ Clear Out, #1281, 1967 (Bendable Leg Francie and Casey), left with gray/blue stripes $120.00, right with more intense blue stripes $140.00.

◆ Plaid Plans, #1767, 1970, missing green scarf (Hair Happenin's Francie), variations with or without green, each outfit $65.00.

◆ **Slacks 'N Cap, pak, 1970 (blouse of the same material belongs to Somethin' Else, #1219, 1969), each $30.00/$45.00.**

◆ **Two Corduroy Capes, #1764, 1970, cape with blue boots (Twiggy and Hair Happenin's Francie), each $25.00.**
◆ **Two Snappy Snoozers, #1238, 1970, different jackets, (Malibu Francie and Casey), each $25.00.**
◆ **Pretty Power, #1512, 1970, Sears, skirt material from Confetti Cutie, Sears, 1968, Orange Zip, Sears, 1968, and other fabric, each piece $20.00.**

◆ **Slack Suit, #3276, 1972 (Bendable Leg Francie and Casey) sitting U.S. version, $45.00; standing German version made of cotton, $80.00.**

◆ **Two Ice Skating, #7845, 1974 (Twist Francie dolls), each $35.00.**
◆ **Three Western Wild, pak, 1970, each $25.00/$45.00.**

Skipper and Ricky

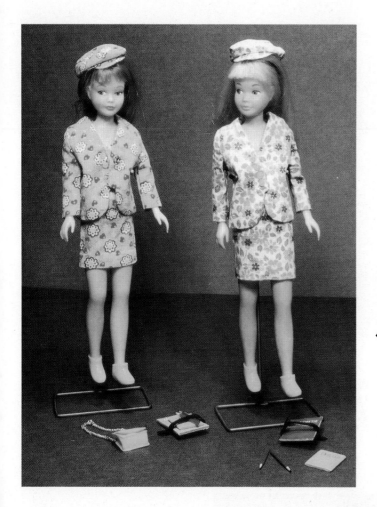

◆ Hearts 'N Flowers, #1945, 1967 (Twist and Bendable Leg Skipper dolls), left $100.00, right $180.00.

◆ Posy Party, #1955, 1968 (Twist Skipper), light version $45.00, darker $65.00.
◆ School's Cool, #1976, 1969 (Twist Skipper), dress on hanger $65.00, regular edition $45.00.

◆ **Summer Slacks, pak, 1968 (Skooter, Bendable Leg Skooter, and first Skipper), various fabrics, right package from Warm 'N Wonderful, #1959, 1967, left standing material, Sears Pretty Power, #1512, 1970, each $25.00/$45.00.**

◆ **Young Ideas, Sears, 1970 (Bendable Leg, Pose 'N Play, and Twist Skipper dolls), left blouse is a replacement, each coat $30.00, each outfit $55.00.**

◆ Budding Beauty, #1731,
1969 (Twist and Bendable
Leg Skipper dolls), left
$20.00, center $30.00, right
$70.00.

◆ Super Slacks, #1736, 1970 (Twist Skipper dolls), left $35.00, right with
unusual yellow lace $45.00.

◆ **Young Ideas, Sears, 1970 (Twist and Living Skipper dolls, Fluff) (the hat belongs to a Mattel Liddle Kiddles doll), each ensemble $25.00.**

◆ **The Slumber Party, pak, 1970 (two Skipper dolls and Skooter), each $15.00.**

◆ **Check the Slacks, pak, 1970, red $15.00/$35.00, black/white $30.00/ $50.00.**
◆ **Lullaby Lime, #3473, 1971 (Malibu Skipper), $20.00/$55.00, nightgown with green straps $30.00.**

From Europe:
◆ **#9931, 1972, $30.00/$45.00.**
◆ **Huebsch in Karos, #7250, 1975, $30.00/$45.00.**

◆ **Two All Over Felt outfits, #3476, 1971 (Twist Skipper dolls), light color $60.00, dark version $100.00.**

◆ **Twice as Nice, #1735, 1970 (Twist Skipper, Fluff), pink $45.00, orange $90.00.**

◆ **Long 'N Short, #3478, 1971 (pink skin Bendable Leg Skooter, Fluff), left $35.00, right $45.00.**

Sold in Germany:
- **Mollig Warm, #2286, 1978, $50.00.**
- **Outfit from about 1976, $30.00.**
  (Two Partytime Skipper dolls.)

• **Huebsch Kombiniert from Germany,**
#2285, 1978 (Funtime Skipper), $60.00.

◆ #1946, 1981 (Sea Lovin' Skipper
and Malibu Skipper), each $5.00.

◆ European outfit for Sweetheart Skipper, 1988, #5886, $15.00/$25.00.

Best Buy outfits:

- ◆ Two #2234, 1978 (Sea Lovin' Skipper), green $20.00, red $7.00/$12.00.
- ◆ #2235, 1978 (Partytime Skipper), floral dress $20.00, boxed dress $7.00/$12.00.

- ◆ **Two European outfits for Sweetheart Skipper, 1988, #5884 and #5883 each $15.00/$25.00.**

◆ **European outfit for Sweetheart Skipper, 1988, note the fur coat variations (with and without pink), #5876, each $15.00/ $25.00.**

◆ **Two European outfits for Sweetheart Skipper, 1988, #5882 and #5883, each $15.00/$25.00.**

♦ **Ricky outfits: two Lights Out, #1501, 1956, left $35.00/$60.00, right
$50.00/$90.00.**

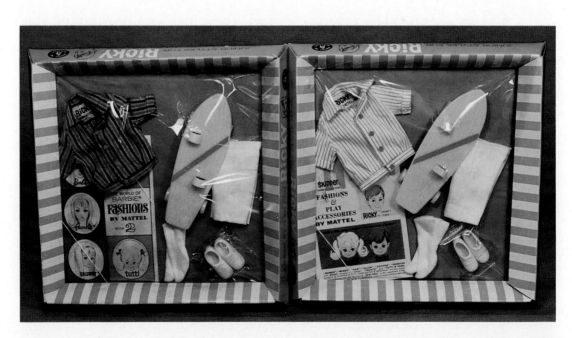

♦ **Ricky outfits: two Skateboard Sets, #1505, dark suit using Sunday Suit
(#1503, 1966) material $90.00/$130.00, regular version $40.00/$65.00.**

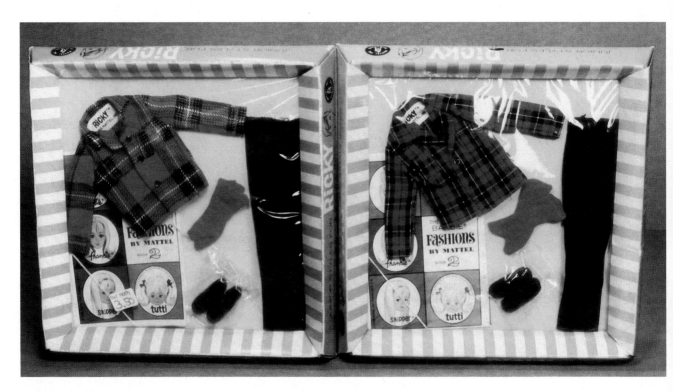

◆ **Ricky outfits: Let's Explore, #1506, 1966, left $50.00/$80.00, right different fabric shirt, $60.00/$100.00.**

Tutti
and Todd

♦ **Skippin' Rope, #3604, 1966 (Chris, Tutti), red version $35.00, white version $55.00.**

♦ **Top: Come to my Party, #3607, 1967, $45.00 (Tutti).**
  ♦ **German Schulausflug, #8466, 1971, $50.00 (Tutti).**
  ♦ **Two versions of Ich geh spielen from Germany, #8593, 1974, each $45.00 (Tutti and Carla).**
♦ **Bottom: Clowning Around, #3606, 1966, $65.00 (Tutti).**
  ♦ **Birthday Beauty, #3617, 1967, $30.00 (Tutti).**
  ♦ **Flower Girl, #3615, 1967, $50.00 (Chris).**

◆ **Two Walkin' My Dolly sets, #3552, 1966, (3 Tutti dolls), left $180.00, center $125.00/$250.00 (prices with accessories). German Ich gen spazieren, #8591, 1974, $50.00.**

◆ **Left from Germany: Two Eingeladen zum Geburtstag outfits, #8505 (Tutti and Chris), blue version $100.00, green version $70.00.**
◆ **Right: Two Let's Play Barbie sets, #3608, 1967 (Tutti dolls), left dress with material from Let's Play House, #1932, 1966, $200.00, right outfit $160.00.**

♦ **Tutti in the German outfit Grosse Reise, #8503, 1972, $70.00. It came with the same case as Let's Play Barbie. Same fabric as Skipper Wooly Winner, #1746, 1970, $60.00.**

♦ **Tutti in Hosenanzug from Germany, #7982, 1975, $70.00. Same material as Mini-Chex, #1209, 1968, $40.00. Note Francie doll's unusual hairdo, possibly prototype, $200.00.**

♦ **German Tutti Im Kindergarten, #9478, 1977, with variation top, $30.00/$50.00 each.**

◆ **Top: Ship Shape, #3602, 1966, $40.00 (Tutti).**
  ◆ **Sand Castle, #3606, 1966, $50.00. (Chris).**
  ◆ **Plantin' Posies, #3609, 1967, $65.00 (Tutti).**
  ◆ **German Schiff Ahoi, #8386, 1971, $40.00 (Chris).**
  ◆ **Sea-Shore Shorties (missing ball), #3614, 1968, $60.00 (Chris).**
  ◆ **German Sonntagsausflug, #8388, 1971, $60.00 (Tutti).**
◆ **Bottom: German Grosse Ferien, #8463, 1971, $80.00 (blue eyed Todd, may be a Liddle Kiddles head on a Todd body).**
  ◆ **German Pulli und Hose, #8595, 1973, $45.00 (Todd).**
  ◆ **German Zum Spielplatz, #8596, 1973, $50.00 (Todd).**
  ◆ **German Mein roter Mantel, #8464, 1971, pants belong to #8502, $45.00.**
  ◆ **German Schneefloeckchen, #8504, 1974, $90.00 (Chris).**
  ◆ **German Bequem und praktisch, #8502, 1972, $40.00 (Tutti).**
  ◆ **German Ich geh spazieren, #8465, 1971, $40.00 (Tutti).**

All outfits from Germany:
◆ **Top: Regentropfen, #8594, 1974, $30.00/$60.00.**
  ◆ **Ausflug, #8597, 1973, same fabric used for Mod Hair Ken from the same year, $60.00/$100.00.**
  ◆ **Spielkleid, #8385, 1972, $45.00/$75.00.**
◆ **Bottom: Three Blue Jeans mit Ringelpulli outfits, #8592, 1974 (notice Tutti in a top from The Combo #1215, 1968, fabric), each $45.00/$70.00.**
  ◆ **Geburtstagsparty, #8389, 1971, $45.00/$75.00.**

- **From Germany, on top: Fuer kuehle Tage, #7971, 1975, $30.00/$50.00.**
  - **Ich geh schlafen, #7981, 1974 (Tutti), $40.00.**
  - **Mein neuer Mantel, #7980, 1974, $40.00/$70.00.**
- **Bottom: Ausflug, #7969, 1975, (Chris) $35.00.**
  - **Regenmantel, #7967, 1975, $50.00/30.00.**
  - **Unknown Tutti outfit from Bells material (#1275, 1967) Carla accompanied by a stuffed elephant from Barbie doll's Room Fulls Studio Bedroom, $80.00.**

German:
- **Top: Neue Jeansmode, #7483, 1976, $30.00/$50.00.**
  - **Huebsch zur Schule, #7484, 1976, $30.00/$50.00.**
  - **Carla in Grosse Ferien, #7480, 1976, $40.00.**
  - **Gut angezogen, #7973, 1975, $30.00/$50.00.**
- **Bottom: Zum Spielplatz, #7479, 1976, $40.00/$60.00.**
  - **Ferienzeit, #7478, 1976 (Tutti), $40.00.**
  - **Grosse Ferien, #7482, 1976, $30.00/$50.00.**
  - **Huebsch angezogen, #7986, 1975, $30.00/$50.00.**

Tutti
and Todd

German:
- **Top: Sport-Fan, #7987, 1975, $35.00/$55.00.**
  - **Zum Spielplatz, #7485, 1976, $30.00/$50.00.**
  - **Ausflug, #7985, 1975, $30.00/$50.00.**
- **Bottom: Zum Spielplatz, #7479, 1976, $30.00/$50.00.**
  - **Ferienzeit, #7478, 1976, $30.00/$50.00.**
  - **Huebsch angezogen, #7986, 1975, $30.00/$50.00.**

German:
- **Top: Zum Spielplatz, #2188, 1978, $25.00/$40.00.**
  - **Kingergeburtstag/Ringbearer, #9479, 1977, $80.00/$120.00.**
  - **Neue Jeansmode, #9481, 1977, $25.00/$40.00.**
- **Bottom: Karo-Mode, #9480, 1977, $25.00/$40.00.**
  - **Auf grosser Reise, #2191, 1978, $25.00/$40.00.**
  - **Schulanfang, #8913, 1980, $35.00/$55.00.**

German:
- ◆ Top: Grosse Ferien, #2657, 1979, $25.00/$40.00.
  - ◆ Baseball, #2655, 1979, $40.00/$65.00.
  - ◆ Vatis Helfer/firefighter, #2654, $40.00/$70.00.
- ◆ Bottom: Spaziergang, #2652, 1979, $30.00/$50.00.
  - ◆ Sportsfreund/Cyclist, #8914, 1980, $40.00/$60.00.
  - ◆ Cowboy, #8915, $45.00/$65.00.

German:
- ◆ Top: Warm angezogen, #9482, 1977, $25.00/$45.00.
  - ◆ Kingergarten, #2656, 1979, $25.00/$40.00.
  - ◆ Ausflug, #2190, 1978, $25.00/$40.00.
- ◆ Bottom: Two Anuschka outfits, #2187, 1978 (Chris and Tutti), $35.00.
- ◆ Turnerin/Gymnast, #8948, 1980, $25.00/$50.00.
- ◆ U.S. Puddle Jumpers, #3601, 1966 (Tutti), $10.00.
- ◆ Drachensteigen, #2189, 1978, $60.00.

Tutti
and Todd

German:
- **Top: Blumenmaedchen/Flowergirl, #2651, 1979, $30.00/$50.00.**
  - **Sonntagskleid, #2650, 1979, out of Quick Curl Barbie material, $50.00/$70.00.**
  - **Festlich angezogen, #9475, 1977, $35.00/$55.00.**
- **Bottom: Kindergeburtstag, #2186, 1977, (Chris) $35.00.**
  - **Kingerbeburtstag, #7481, 1976, (Chris) $30.00.**
  - **Zirkusstar, #8946, 1980, $50.00/$70.00.**
  - **Zirkusclown, #8912, 1980, (Todd) $50.00/$70.00.**
  - **Gartenfest, #7970, (Tutti) $35.00.**

German:
- **Top: Im Kindergarten, #9478, 1977, $30.00/$50.00.**
  - **Nostalgie, #8949, 1980, $30.00/$40.00.**
  - **Gute Nacht, #2185, 1977, with a cute pink bear, $40.00/$60.00.**
- **Bottom: Spielplatz, #2653, 1979, $30.00/$50.00.**
  - **Am Strand, #2184, 1978, $30.00/$50.00.**
  - **Spielkleid, #8947, 1980 (Chris), $30.00.**
  - **Huebsch und praktisch, #9477, 1977, with a cookbook, $40.00/$70.00.**

Right from the beginning in 1959 Barbie was heavily promoted. Pink silhouette box Barbie dolls came fully dressed and were part of a counter display. They were not intended to be sold. After the doll or outfit was no longer produced a few of them were given away to customers. Shamefully most boxes were thrown away by the merchants. Most of the dolls in these boxes are No. 1 – 3 Barbie dolls, but a No. 4 has been found, too. Up to now, 18 differently dressed pink box dolls are known. The stock numbers are the same as the ones of the 900 Series outfits the dolls are modeling except that the numbers start with an eight (#864 for a doll in a Gay Parisienne outfit that normally has the number #964).

◆ **Pink silhouette box No. 1 Barbie in Gay Parisienne, #864, 1959, $6,500.00.**

◆ **Pink silhouette box No. 3 Barbie in Sweater Girl, #876, 1960 (this doll has unusual orange lips that match the color of her outfit), $2,800.00.**

Dressed Box Dolls

In 1963 Mattel began selling dressed dolls to the public. Available in special boxes with an extra clear lid were Ponytail and Bubble Cut Barbie dolls, Ken with painted hair, and straight leg Skipper. Barbie dolls wearing outfits with wider skirts came with an additional panty (as sold with Undergarment, #919, 1959).

- ♦ **Dressed box Bubble Cut Barbie in After Five, #934, 1963, $500.00.**
- ♦ **Dressed box Bubble Cut Barbie in Golden Elegance, #992, 1963, $550.00.**
- ♦ **Dressed box Ponytail Barbie, in Senior Prom, #951, 1963, $650.00.**

- ♦ **Dressed box Ken in Arabian Night, #774, 1964, $450.00.**
- ♦ **Dressed box Ken in Ken in Holland, #777, 1964, $450.00.**
- ♦ **Dressed box Bubble Cut Barbie in Guinevere, #873, 1964, $550.00.**
- ♦ **Dressed box Skipper in Flower Girl, #1904, 1964, $350.00.**

◆ **Sew Free Fashion Fun Display, 1965, $100.00 (without outfits).**

◆ **Displays for Skipper and Barbie fashions, late 60s, each box $70.00 (empty).**

European Displays

Displays found in Germany unless otherwise noted.

◆ Gartenparty, large display, mid 70s. Material: sprayed rubber on plywood, all food and the oven are made out of mold injected rubber. Left over dolls from earlier years were stapled (brutally) into the wood, $800.00.

◆ St. Tropez, again a large display found in Germany, same material as the previous display, $800.00.

◆ Very large display (about 4 feet wide and 16 inches deep) from France, has mold injected rubber stones and a wooden fence next to an actual piece of tree mounted into the plywood. Note the realistic spraying of dust on Skipper and the horse, Dancer, after their ride. Late 70s, $600.00.

◆ Carousel from 1978 with electrical movement, $650.00.

♦ **Mode-Collection display, mid 80s. A motor inside moves a saucer that holds three Barbie dolls (outfits replaced), $350.00.**

♦ **Fashion Collection display, mid 1980s (outfits are replacements). Note the unusual mannequins. $500.00.**

◆ **Rock Star (Rockers) display from 1986 with lights,**
$350.00.

◆ **Mannequin (Magic Moves)**
display, 1986, $150.00.

European
Displays

◆ **First Happy Holidays display (with lights), 1989, $500.00.**

◆ **Second Happy Holidays display (with lights), 1990, $350.00.**

♦ **Büro und Wohn Set promotes City Barbie, electric. Two pictures slide over another, $250.00.**

The following displays are made of cardboard. They were delivered flat to the merchant and had to be folded into shape. Usually included were two dolls or one doll and an animal plus stand(s).

♦ **Sun Charm display, 1990, $200.00.**

◆ **Safari (Animal Lovin') display, 1989, $200.00.**

◆ **SuperStar display, 1989, $200.00.**

◆ **Dream Dance (Dance Magic) display, 1990, $200.00.**

◆ **Hawaii (Hawaiian Fun) Barbie display, dolls are out of cardboard, 1991, $80.00.**

German
Signs

◆ **City Barbie sign,**
1985, $25.00.

◆ **Rock Stars (Rockers)**
sign, 1986, $25.00.

◆ Large Haute Couture sign, 1987, $40.00.

◆ Maritim (Sea Lovin') sign,
1985, $20.00.

◆ Meine erste Barbie-Set (My First Barbie Set) sign, 1987,
$35.00.

◆ **Sign to promote new outfits.
With every purchase a free kit
for one cardboard suitcase was
given away, 1989. Sign
$100.00, kit $15.00.**

◆ **Sun Charm sign, 1990, $25.00.**

♦ German booklet
from 1964. Note the
unusual format (to
fit into a Barbie box)
and the "Turtle
mark" on the cover
(this company dis-
tributed Barbie dolls
in the early 60s in
Germany), $80.00.

♦ Booklets from
late 60s to mid
70s, each $30.00
to $80.00.

♦ Barbie Journals
from 80s, each
$5.00.

Gift Sets

During 60s and early 70s Mattel released over 60 different Gift Sets. The earlier ones consist of outfit(s) from the regular line and up to four dolls (sometimes only outfits).

From the mid 60s on the Gift Sets came with special and exclusive outfits. Sometimes they are color variations of existing dresses, most of the time they are newly designed outfits.

All the U.S. Gift Sets from this time were department store specials from either Sears, Penneys, or Wards. Up to now only one European Gift Set has been found. It was sold in France about 1972.

Dolls from the regular line were used for the Gift Sets. The only exceptions are Living Barbie and Skipper from the Action Accents Gift Set and Very Best Velvet Living Skipper Set. These dolls were made in Japan instead of in Taiwan (like all the other Living dolls).

♦ **Wedding Party Gift Set, #1017, 1964 (missing little yellow pillow with ring), $600.00/$2,000.00.**

◆ **Pep Rally Set, #1022, 1964,**
$150.00/$450.00.

◆ **Mix 'N Match Gift Set, #857, 1963, $180.00/$775.00.**

◆ **Skipper Party Time Set, #1021, 1964, $130.00/$400.00.**

◆ **Skipper On Wheels Set, #1032, 1965, Sears, $100.00/$250.00.**

♦ **Skooter Cut 'n Button Set, #1036, 1965, Sears, $200.00/$320.00. The gift set came with one Skooter. The pictured background belongs to the Barbie Little Theatre.**

♦ **Two left outfits are from the Barbie Hostess Gift Set, #1034, 1965, $700.00/ $2,500.00. The dolls on the right wear matching outfits from the regular line (Invitation to Tea, #1632, 1965 and Barbie Learns to Cook, #1634, 1965) each $200.00. Not all accessories are pictured.**

◆ **Braniff Gift Set, Wards, not made by Mattel but considered a Barbie collectible, 1967, never removed from box $2,000.00. Out of box: Serving Dress $200.00, blue Hostess Pajamas $200.00, Boarding Outfit (helmet not pictured) $500.00, Raspberry Suit (not pictured) $300.00.**

◆ **Color Magic Fashion Designer Set, #4040, 1966, Sears $350.00/$500.00.**

◆ **Color Magic Fashion Designer Set outfits, each outfit $100.00.**

◆ **Color Magic Fashion Designer Set outfit, $100.00.**

◆ **Pink Premiere Set, #1596, 1969, Penneys, $300.00/$500.00.**
◆ **Golden Grove Set, #1593, 1969, Sears, $300.00/$550.00.**

- Nite Lightning Stacey Gift Set, #1591, 1969, Sears, $300.00/$900.00. (the purse pictured is an addition).
- Beautiful Blues Set, #3303, 1967, Sears, $400.00/$950.00.

- Dinner Dazzle Sets, #1551, 1967, Sears. Left, regular version, $350.00/ $600.00. Right, color variation, $550.00/$900.00 (note the unusual hairdo of the sitting doll, prototype?).

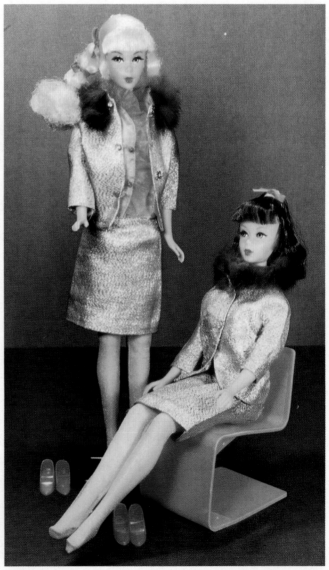

♦ **PJ Swingin' In Silver Set, #1588, 1970, Penneys, $250.00/$550.00.**
♦ **Silver 'N Satin Set, #1552, 1968, Penneys, $450.00/$700.00.**

♦ **Right: Fabulous Formal Set, #1595, 1969, Sears (Ken not pictured), $450.00/$800.00.**
♦ **Left: the matching regular line outfit Romantic Ruffles, #1871, 1969, $100.00.**

- ◆ **Stripes Are Happening Stacey Set,**
  #1545, 1968, Sears, $300.00/$550.00.
- ◆ **Twinkle Town Set, #1866, 1969, Sears,**
  $400.00/$850.00 (this Gift Set came
  with a regular line outfit and a rare
  color variation swim suit).

- ◆ **Bright and Breezy Skipper set, #1590,**
  1969, Sears, $230.00/$400.00.
- ◆ **Travel in Style set, #1544, 1967,**
  Sears (pictured without blue stock-
  ings), $280.00/$550.00.

◆ **Very Best Velvet Living Skipper Set, #1586, 1970, Sears, came with a Living Skipper made in Japan (note the slightly different expression and hair quality), $400.00/$700.00.**

◆ **Perfectly Pretty Skipper Set, #1546, 1969, Sears (hat not pictured), $250.00/$400.00.**

◆ **Chris Funtimer Gift Set, #3301, 1967, Sears (came with one doll only), $200.00/$350.00.**

◆ Casey Goes Casual Set, #3304, 1967, Sears (one doll only), $300.00/$450.00.

◆ Francie and Her Swingin' Separates, #1042, 1966, Sears (one doll only), $300.00/$500.00.

◆ **Rise and Shine Francie Set, #1194, 1971, Sears, $300.00/$450.00.**

◆ **Action Accents Living Barbie Set, #1585, 1970, Sears, came with a Living Barbie made in Japan, $350.00/ $750.00.**
◆ **On left is an unusual brunette Live Action PJ (possibly a fake).**

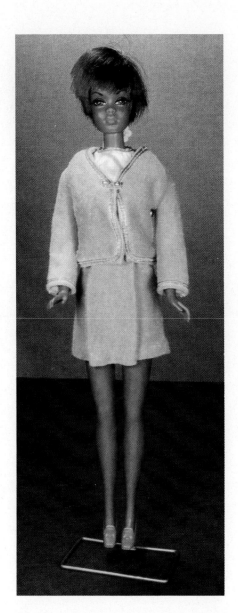

◆ **Talking Julia Gift Set, 1969,
Sears, $300.00/$650.00.**

◆ **Perfectly Plaid Set, #1193, 1971, Sears
(replaced hat), $200.00/$400.00.**
◆ **Talking Barbie Gift Set, 1970, Sears,
$250.00/$450.00.**

◆ **Left: Furry Friends Jamie Gift Set, #1584, 1970, Sears, $250.00/$400.00.**
◆ **Center and right: Strollin' in Style Jamie Gift Set, #1247, 1971, Sears (one doll only), $350.00/$550.00.**

◆ **Fashion 'N Motion PJ set, #1508, 1971, Sears, $180.00/$350.00.**
◆ **Sunshine Special Fluff Set, #1249, 1971, Sears, $150.00/$350.00.**

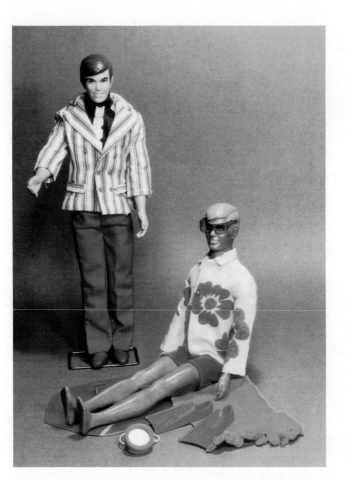

◆ **Red, White, and Wild Ken Set, #1589, 1969, Sears (the jacket is original, pants, top, and tie may be replaced), $180.00/$400.00.**
◆ **Surf's Up Ken Set, #1248, 1971, Sears $100.00/$250.00.**

◆ **Pose 'N Play Skipper and her Swing-A-Rounder Gym Set, #1179, 1972, $70.00/$200.00.**

◆ **Barbie et Ken et leurs nouveaux habillages** set from France, about 1972 (outfits resewn to replacement card), $250.00/$800.00.

◆ **Four cases made in France, late 60s, each $150.00.**

◆ **Left: Two Barbie cases made in Germany, each $140.00.**
◆ **Right top: case made in Canada, $90.00.**
◆ **Right bottom: Ken and Allan case made in France, $300.00.**

- Skipper case made in Germany, #4966, $35.00.
- Barbie case made in Canada, $90.00.

- Top: Tutti case made in Germany (the U.S. version is pink), $45.00.
- Bottom: Two Skipper and Skooter cases made in France, each $100.00.

◆ **Magic Moves Barbie case from Canada, 1986, $15.00.**

◆ **Two Tutti cases with original hangers, each $45.00 (without Chris) (notice the train's destination is Hamburg).**

♦ Villa Barbie made in Germany,
  #0-1105, 1971, $150.00
  (without Twist Barbie).

- ◆ **German horse stable for Equestrienne Barbie, #90-9902, 1977, $60.00.**
- ◆ **Brown horse with molded hair: Dancer, #92-7385, 1977, $35.00.**
- ◆ **White horse with real hair: Dallas, #3468, 1983, $25.00.**

◆ **Dream Carriage, #5493, 1983, was sold in Canada with two horses, $150.00, in Europe without horses, $100.00.**

◆ **Mr. Bobbie from Germany, #6252, 1989, the same dog was used in the U.S. as part of The Heart Family line, $35.00.**

◆ **Barbie and Ken hangers made in Canada, 1963, $25.00.**

◆ **Italian Barbie masks for children, late 80s, each $40.00.**

Author's

Collection

I caught the "Barbie-Virus" in 1980. Since then, not a day goes by without me enjoying these dolls; hunting for them; contacting other collectors; arranging and visiting exhibitions, meetings, and shows; writing Barbie newsletters, articles, and books.

I cannot say how many Barbie dolls and outfits are in my collection. I stopped counting when I reached the 2,000 doll mark several years ago.

No matter how big my collection grows, my wish list doesn't seem to become smaller. With all the variations, foreign dolls, and licensed merchandise there is no danger of running out of Barbie items to collect.

My favorites are early Barbie dolls and Lillis, as well as outfits from the 60s. But I also become weak when I see some of the gorgeous new collector Barbie dolls.

Schroeder's ANTIQUES Price Guide

. . . is the #1 best-selling antiques & collectibles value guide on the market today, and here's why . . .

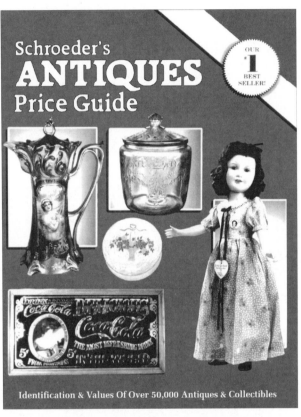

Schroeder's **ANTIQUES** Price Guide

OUR #1 BEST SELLER!

Identification & Values Of Over 50,000 Antiques & Collectibles

8½ x 11, 608 Pages, $14.95

- *More than 300 advisors, well-known dealers, and top-notch collectors work together with our editors to bring you accurate information regarding pricing and identification.*

- *More than 45,000 items in almost 500 categories are listed along with hundreds of sharp original photos that illustrate not only the rare and unusual, but the common, popular collectibles as well.*

- *Each large close-up shot shows important details clearly. Every subject is represented with histories and background information, a feature not found in any of our competitors' publications.*

- *Our editors keep abreast of newly developing trends, often adding several new categories a year as the need arises.*

If it merits the interest of today's collector, you'll find it in Schroeder's. And you can feel confident that the information we publish is up to date and accurate. Our advisors thoroughly check each category to spot inconsistencies, listings that may not be entirely reflective of market dealings, and lines too vague to be of merit. Only the best of the lot remains for publication.

Without doubt, you'll find
SCHROEDER'S ANTIQUES PRICE GUIDE
the only one to buy for
reliable information and values.

COLLECTOR BOOKS
A Division of Schroeder Publishing Co., Inc.